A Profile of the Global Airline Industry

A Profile of the Global Airline Industry

Kent N. Gourdin

 BUSINESS EXPERT PRESS

A Profile of the Global Airline Industry

First published in 2016 by
Business Expert Press, LLC
222 East 46th Street, New York, NY 10017
www.businessexpertpress.com

ISBN-13: 978-1-60649-554-4 (paperback)
ISBN-13: 978-1-60649-555-1 (e-book)

Business Expert Press Industry Profiles Collection

Collection ISSN: 2331-0065 (print)
Collection ISSN: 2331-0073 (electronic)

Cover and interior design by Exeter Premedia Services Private Ltd.,
Chennai, India

First edition: 2016

10 9 8 7 6 5 4 3 2 1

Printed in the United States of America.

Abstract

The airline industry is one of the most fascinating in the world, with roots going back to the earliest years of the 20th century. Not long after the Wright brothers flew successfully for the first time in 1903, interest in aviation for military and commercial purposes began. In the late teens, the U.S. government began offering potentially lucrative airmail contracts to start-up air carriers, who competed vigorously for them often with disastrous results. Despite the rocky start, the carriers persevered and, by the 1930s, were beginning to look like the companies we see today. This book will provide the reader insight into the nature of the airlines and why companies promulgate the strategies they do. First, the history of commercial air services will be examined, with an initial focus on the United States. After this background, airline operations around the world will be compared and the different types of carriers that comprise the industry will be discussed. Next, the reader will learn about important uncontrollable outside forces (fuel costs, terrorism, economic conditions, etc.) that can have dramatic and potentially devastating impacts on an airline. A discussion of economic regulation and deregulation will follow to help the reader understand the impact of both legislate actions on the carriers operating today. Finally, in the face of expected increases in the demand for the global movement of passengers and cargo, future opportunities and challenges facing the airline industry will be presented.

Keywords

airlines, air carriers, air transportation, air travel, deregulation, economic, logistics

Contents

Acknowledgments

I would like to thank my wife, Susan, for all of her help and assistance with proofing multiple drafts as well as for her valuable input on content. In addition, our daughter, Maggie, contributed her good humor and many cogent comments that together made the entire process much more enjoyable. Thanks to you both for your support.

CHAPTER 1

Introduction

Background

The airline industry is one of the most fascinating in the world, with roots going back to the earliest years of the 20th century. Not long after the Wright brothers flew successfully for the first time in 1903, interest in aviation for military and commercial purposes began. Following World War I, the U.S. government began offering potentially lucrative airmail contracts to start-up air carriers, who competed vigorously for them often with disastrous results. Given the crude aircraft, lack of navigation and weather forecasting services, and poor pilot training, crashes became the rule rather than the exception. Despite the rocky start, the carriers persevered and by the 1930s were beginning to look like the companies we see today. In fact, competition in the United States became so severe that the government created the Civil Aeronautics Board (CAB) in 1938 to regulate the business of domestic air travel. The industry worldwide got a tremendous boost after World War II, with the availability of inexpensive military surplus aircraft and a plethora of airfields that could easily be converted to civilian use.

Commercial aviation, both in the United States and abroad, continued to grow during the 1950s, 1960s, and 1970s. By the mid-1970s, Congress decided that economic regulation was no longer necessary and began the process of deregulation by freeing the all-cargo carriers from most CAB oversight in 1977. In 1978, for better or worse, the passenger airlines were deregulated as well.

Deregulation transformed the U.S. airline industry forever. New carriers entered the marketplace, while old ones failed. As the demand for international travel increased, airlines in other countries began to grow as they found ways to successfully compete against what had been an industry largely dominated by U.S. firms. Competition forced managers to adopt cost control measures that seriously degraded service, while more recently rising fuel prices have made profitability even more elusive. Indeed, the carriers well regarded by passengers today are not based in Los Angeles or New York, but rather in Dubai, Singapore, or Germany.

In order to provide insight into the nature of the airlines and why companies promulgate the strategies they do, the history of commercial air services will be examined, with an initial focus on the United States. After this background, airline operations around the world will be compared and the different types of carriers that comprise the industry will be discussed. Next, the reader will learn about important uncontrollable outside forces (fuel costs, terrorism, economic conditions, etc.) that can have dramatic and potentially devastating impacts on an airline. A discussion of economic regulation and deregulation will follow, to help the reader understand the impact of both legislative actions on the carriers operating today. Finally, in the face of expected increases in the demand for the global movement of passengers and cargo, future opportunities and challenges facing the airline industry will be presented.

The Early Years: 1918 to 1938

Commercial aviation in America began in 1918 with the transport of airmail, first by the U.S. Army Air Service and then by the U.S. Post Office, which carried the mail for nine years using its own pilots and airplanes. To say that flying at that time was fraught with danger is an understatement. Thirty-one of the first 40 airmail pilots hired by the government died in crashes.[1] There were no airways, navigational aids, or emergency landing fields; no federal agencies that dealt with civilian flying and no federal laws to regulate it; no standards for aircraft maintenance; and no mechanism for licensing pilots.[2]

Similar developments were occurring in Europe. For many months after the war, normal rail travel in Europe remained problematic and irregular because of the shortage of passenger equipment and the destruction of tracks and bridges. In addition, chaotic political conditions in Central and Eastern Europe often disrupted schedules. The situation opened many possibilities for launching airline routes. Although few airfields existed, aircraft of the postwar era could and did use relatively short sod runways for years, meaning that locating suitable airports near most cities was not the formidable engineering challenge that emerged in subsequent decades. Another factor that emerged as a driver of airline development in Europe was the ongoing need to tie far-flung empires to their respective mother countries. Great Britain, France, and the Netherlands all had colonies around the world; while in the nascent Union of Soviet Socialist Republics (USSR), air transport emerged as an indispensable medium for rapid transportation and a visible means of knitting together sprawling, divergent regions.[3] In fact, the oldest continuously operating airline in the world is the Dutch carrier KLM, which was founded in 1919.[4]

A significant difference between the United States and the rest of the world was that the former relied on the private sector to develop its airlines while virtually every other nation created and operated its own national carrier(s), a fact that continues to impact global commercial aviation to this day.

One factor that quickly became apparent in the United States was that the demand for military aircraft alone could not sustain aircraft manufacturing, which prior to 1917 was virtually nonexistent.[5] After the war, the government was buying fewer planes while commercial flying was virtually nonexistent.[6] As a result, there was no civilian market for planes. The government's decision to sell its surplus aircraft to civilians at cheap rates made an impossible situation even worse. The availability of inexpensive planes did lure many people into the air transport business, but those enterprises proved too precarious either to provide reliable transport service or to serve as a market for planes. For example, in the United States, there were 88 airline operators in 1921 and 129 in 1923, yet the latter figure included only 17 of the original 88. While some companies managed to eke out a thin existence with a plane or two, as late as 1924 the nation still did not have a single regularly scheduled air transport line.[7]

Structure Emerges

The event that brought order to the chaos was the passage of the Air Commerce Act of 1926. Championed by then-Secretary of Commerce

Herbert Hoover, the act's impact was enormous. During the period from 1922 to 1926, the nation added only 369 miles of regular air service operated by private enterprise and 3,000 miles of airmail lines run by the post office that did not carry passengers or express. By 1929, there were 25,000 miles of government-improved airways of which 14,000 were lighted with beacons; 1,000 airports built and 1,200 in progress; 6,400 licensed planes making 25,000,000 miles in regular flights annually; and a manufacturing output of 7,500 planes a year.[8] In fact, the act paved the way for the formation of three of today's four largest U.S. airlines: Delta, which started as a crop-dusting operation in 1924 and carried its first domestic passengers in 1929; United Airlines which began in 1931; and American in 1930. Of course, there were many others as well (Northwest, 1926; Pan American, 1927; Eastern, 1927; Trans World Airlines [TWA], 1930; Braniff, 1931; Continental, 1934; National, 1934), although these have all failed or been assimilated by other carriers.[9] Perhaps the greatest impact of the act was to establish a model of private industry and public promotion working together to establish a strong U.S. airline industry responsive to the needs of the nation.

Naturally, all these new airlines were trying to compete with each other during one of the worst depressions ever to occur in the United States. Recall that there was no government oversight of the industry, so managers were free to make whatever business decisions they thought best, with little regard for the stability of the industry. Congress had established a precedent of imposing economic regulation on the railroad, pipeline, and trucking industries engaged in interstate commerce because they viewed such a move as being in the public interest. The airlines were brought under that regulatory umbrella in 1938. While the topic of economic regulation will be covered in a later chapter, the CAB was created to stabilize the fledgling airline industry by controlling prices and limiting competition. One goal at the time was to encourage the spread of commercial air services across the nation. Of course, the airlines only wanted to serve routes that they knew would be profitable, so the agency utilized the award of operating authorities (i.e., permission) to ensure the public need for air services would be met. Essentially, carriers were forced to serve both money-making and money-losing routes, with the earnings from the former offsetting the losses of the latter so that overall the carrier made a profit. By limiting the number of certificates awarded to serve profitable or high-demand routes and increasing those for unprofitable or low-demand ones, the CAB limited competition on the former and increased it on the latter. The impact on fares was predictable: higher prices where competition was restricted and lower where it was forced.

Expansion Abroad

Global expansion on any meaningful level was constrained by the lack of suitable aircraft and infrastructure. Pan American established itself as an international carrier with a short-lived passenger service from Key West to Havana in 1927. The carrier proved so adept at winning federal airmail contracts that services throughout the Caribbean quickly followed.[10] However, crossing the Atlantic and the Pacific Oceans proved much more challenging. The Atlantic routes had to be via intermediate points, either by the northern countries, or via island hopping points in the Central Atlantic. The problem thus became one of territorial sovereignty. Great Britain, for example, through its Commonwealth connection to Canada stood in the way of the initial segment of the Great Circle route eastwards from New York. The British were not anxious to allow the Americans to start a service before they were ready themselves. Similarly, France had secured exclusive landing rights to the Azores, the vital halfway point in the middle of the Atlantic, by an agreement with Portugal, which controlled the islands. Denmark still extended its political domain to the Faröe Islands, Iceland, and Greenland, and thus controlled the northern perimeter.[11]

There were actually fewer operational and political problems growing across the Pacific. Initial efforts focused on securing a Great Circle route from New York to Tokyo via Canada, Alaska, and the Soviet Union, but the Soviets refused to allow U.S. carriers to transit its airspace because America continued to withhold diplomatic recognition. All interest then shifted to the Central Pacific. The weather was better, but more importantly, the United States controlled vital territories like Hawaii, Midway and Wake Islands, Guam, and the Philippines, which meant that trans-Pacific air services could be stitched together without asking for permission from any foreign government. One big problem remained, aside from the challenge of developing an aircraft capable of profitably flying between San Francisco and Honolulu: the lack of infrastructure between Hawaii and Manila. Pan American faced the challenge head-on and built these resources itself. It leased a ship, organized supplies and equipment, and dispatched it with 44 airline technicians and 74 construction staff. The cargo included enough material to construct two complete villages and five air bases (including hotel accommodations for passengers and crew), the most important of which were at Midway and Wake Islands, tiny specks of U.S. territory in the middle of the Pacific where two flying boat bases were blasted out of the coral. All this work was completed in mid-1935, with scheduled airmail service starting in November of that year and passenger service a year later.[12] A few statistics on the first flight from San Francisco to Manila: one-way fare was $799, the equivalent of $13,895 in 2014; total flight time was 59 hours, 48 minutes (21 hours from San Francisco to Honolulu alone); total elapsed time was seven days.[13]

World War II and the Postwar Years: 1939 to 1958

Unfortunately, as the 1930s wore on, the threat of war in both Europe and the Pacific became more acute, slowing further developments in the industry. Pan American started transatlantic services in 1939, only to curtail them a few months later. By the time the United States actually entered the conflict in December of 1941, international commercial flights had virtually ceased as did casual air travel within the United States. The Army's Air Transport Command was formed in 1942 to coordinate the transport of aircraft, cargo, and personnel throughout the country and around the world. The Air Transport Command contracted with airlines to fly wherever they were needed. Pan American's vast overseas experience became an especially valuable asset. Unfortunately, other airlines also received overseas routes, only to become Pan American's postwar competitors: Northwest flew to Alaska and the Pacific; United to Hawaii and the Pacific; Eastern and Braniff to Latin America; TWA across the Atlantic; and American to Africa, India, and China.[14]

By 1944, the outcome of the war was ordained as was the future of air transportation. The allied nations of the world gathered in Chicago to lay the groundwork for postwar international commercial air transport. Fifty-two countries signed the Convention on International Civil Aviation on (ironically) December 7, 1944, an agreement that continues to form the basis for the exchange of air rights between nations to this day.[15] With the plethora of surplus aircraft available and military air bases ripe for conversion to civilian use, the stage was set for international air transportation to grow once the global economy recovered.

The 1950s saw unprecedented growth in the demand for both domestic and overseas air travel. Regulation by the CAB in the United States limited new entrants and pretty much ensured prosperity for what have come to be known as the legacy carriers. There were several systemic events that occurred during this period as well. First, the Civil Reserve Air Fleet (CRAF) was created in 1954 to augment Department of Defense (DOD) airlift requirements when emergency needs exceed the capability of military aircraft. This program, which is still in place today, eliminates the need for a huge investment in military aircraft that (hopefully) will never be needed. The airlines contractually pledge aircraft to the various segments of CRAF, ready for activation when needed. To provide incentives for civil carriers to commit aircraft to the CRAF program and to assure the United States of adequate airlift reserves, the government makes peacetime DOD airlift business (passengers and cargo) available to civilian airlines that offer aircraft to the CRAF.[16] Two other noteworthy events that both occurred in 1958 were the introduction of the first jet-powered transports into scheduled service and the creation of what is known today as the Federal Aviation Administration (FAA) to oversee air traffic control and flight safety issues.

The Calm Before the Storm: 1959 to 1978

This period was one of domestic stability and international growth. Recall that the CAB continued to regulate domestic U.S. competition and fares such that both new entrants and failures of existing airlines were equally rare. Internationally, airlines were still primarily government owned and thus more concerned with expanding their nation's global presence than with profitability (Pan American was also used in this role by the U.S. government, though without any direct support). Thus many countries, even those with no domestic markets, operated subsidized airlines in competition with U.S. carriers, a situation that still exists.

The winds of change began to blow in the mid-1970s when Congress started to question the efficacy of transportation regulation. The feeling was that the time had come to allow market forces to allocate transportation services. With regard to the air transport industry, there was concern that passengers were paying more than they should be and that the carriers were constrained from responding to the changing demands of a mature marketplace. Congress dipped a legislative toe in the water in 1977 by freeing the cargo-only airlines from domestic economic regulation, then committed completely in 1978 by passing the Airline Deregulation Act, which did the same for the passenger carriers as well. The industry has never been the same.

Adapting to the Free Market: 1979 to 1998

Deregulation put the business of air transportation back into the hands of carrier managers. "Normal" corporate decisions related to issues like where to fly, what services to offer, and fares, which since 1938 required CAB vetting, were now (with the exception of some initial limitations on pricing freedom) left up to management. The relaxation of barriers to entry encouraged new carriers to initiate services in competition with the legacy carriers. In other words, airlines were given the ability to succeed or fail without interference from the federal government. Two important caveats must be made before proceeding. First, deregulation applied only to business matters. The government was and still is very much involved in air traffic control, safety, labor, environmental, and antitrust issues pertaining to the airline industry. Second, deregulation was strictly a U.S. phenomenon that only applied to domestic airlines and services; international aviation continued to be strictly controlled.

Competition

Because government barriers to entry were eliminated, there was a dramatic influx of new airlines virtually all of which were competing with the established carriers on the basis of price. In fact, as a group, these new entrants came to be known as no-frills airlines because the low price bought only a seat; everything else was a "frill" that either cost additional money or was eliminated altogether. Pretty much every aspect of flying that passengers were used to fell into this category: complimentary in-flight meals and drinks, pillows and blankets, advance seat selection, and even the ability to book a flight were all viewed as extras. Perhaps the best known of these carriers was People Express, which began service on April 30, 1981 with the strategy of short flights, small fares, no frills, and indirect competition (operating at lesser used airports in the vicinity of large airline hubs).[17] Passengers arrived at the terminal without a reservation and paid onboard the aircraft. There were no assigned seats; if and when the aircraft filled up, those waiting either caught the next flight or made other arrangements. By the end of 1981, over 950,000 passengers had flown on a People Express flight, many of whom had never flown before. The reality was that the fares were often lower than driving or taking the bus. To say their strategy was a success is an understatement. In fact, the airline grew at an astounding rate and, at one point, was the fastest growing company in the nation.[18] Unfortunately, that growth ultimately contributed to their demise, but not before they spawned many imitators who collectively redefined airline competition in the United States.

While People Express instituted a London service as a part of their failed growth strategy, low-fare or low-service air transport was not strictly a U.S. phenomenon. Icelandair began offering transatlantic low-budget flights with single-class seating in the mid-1950s, connecting the United States with Luxembourg via Reykjavik.[19] Laker Airways, a private British carrier that started as an ad-hoc charter airline in 1966, began no-frills scheduled services between London and New York in 1977. Despite the carrier's efforts to expand with similar flights to Australia, Hong Kong, and other U.S. destinations, British regulatory impediments and the recession in early 1980 conspired to push the company into bankruptcy in February 1982.[20]

Fares and Yield Management

A study by the Government Accounting Office (GAO) in 1996 stated that domestic fares overall fell between 1979 and 1994, although the impact across specific airports was not even. For example, of the 112 airports in the study, eight experienced fare increases of more than 20 percent while 14 saw decreases in excess of 20 percent, with the remainder falling somewhere in between.[21] Much of this variation can be attributed to the fact that fares now reflected actual demand such that prices on high-demand routes fell as additional carriers began serving them while those on low-demand routes rose as competition declined, a complete reversal from the situation under regulation. Distance per se became largely irrelevant to the pricing equation, so passengers often realized they were paying higher fares to fly fewer miles, which intuitively seemed wrong even if economic theory says otherwise. In other words, airlines began charging fares based on where and when passengers wanted to travel, thus applying the concept of price elasticity (how sensitive people are to changes in price) to the demand for air travel. A passenger who wants or needs to fly today will be willing pay a very high fare (e.g., a business person), while a leisure traveler will book well in advance to get a lower one. Understanding passengers' demand elasticity allowed the airlines to develop a myriad of fares intended to maximize the revenue on every flight, a practice known as yield or revenue management. Obviously, such a system requires a tremendous amount of historical data, which the legacy airlines had been capturing for years via their proprietary reservations systems. This capability enabled them to compete with the new low-price carriers by selectively lowering fares to match them on the routes where the two competed while continuing to offer their higher service levels.

This same principle has been applied to air freight charges as well. FedEx was originally an overnight service that guaranteed delivery by 10:00 a.m. the next morning and was priced accordingly. In other words, by calling FedEx, customers communicated their urgency of need and consequent willingness to pay the high price. Gradually, FedEx (and, later, UPS) began offering cheaper second- and third-day services, in addition to next-day. This strategy allows the carrier to capture more price-sensitive buyers while, at the same time, better managing their aircraft loads. For example, freight that is identified for three-day service may actually move overnight if the airplane has room, though it will not be delivered until the date paid for by the customer. By the same token, FedEx will even accept cargo for same-day delivery, although in most cases this freight will be put on a scheduled passenger flight. Needless to say, this service is extremely expensive.

Networks

One of the early results of deregulation was the abandonment of unprofitable routes to primarily small communities that the carriers had been forced by the CAB to serve. Many of these towns had enjoyed scheduled, if relatively infrequent, service for decades, so the loss was very traumatic. During the first 10 years of deregulation (the 1980s), the major airlines shifted dramatically from point-to-point to hub-and-spoke route systems. Following the example of prederegulation Delta, which pioneered the concept at Atlanta, the major airlines built up major connecting hubs at what had been principally origin-and-destination airports, such as Charlotte, Dallas, Detroit, Minneapolis, Pittsburgh, and St. Louis. Hubs made possible huge increases in service for two categories of air traveler. First, those living in the hub-airport city gained access to a many more destinations and flights. Second, residents of small cities on the spokes of the hub, who may have lost some point-to-point service, gained access to potentially hundreds of destinations via the hub.[22] In fact, many of these locales actually ended up having better (i.e., more frequent) service then they did prior to 1978. Of course, the major advantage of the hub-and-spoke accrued to the airline because support activities such as catering, maintenance, and fueling could be concentrated at the hub rather than scattered throughout a point-to-point system, thereby lowering costs. In addition, the carrier could operate full but smaller aircraft into and out of the hub, minimizing empty seats.

Operating Costs

The thread running through the discussion about deregulation so far is cost reduction, a topic largely unfamiliar to airline managers used to economic regulation. The rapid market inroads made by innovative low-cost competitors forced a complete overhaul in the way the business was run. The move to hub-and-spoke networks was very much cost driven, as was the elimination of unprofitable routes. The 1980s and 1990s saw the paring of employees and passenger services as labor contracts were renegotiated to lower costs. Many of these changes had a direct and largely negative impact on the in-flight customer experience as passengers still expected preregulation service and postderegulation fares. Aircraft technology emphasized cost savings as well, offering new airliners with better fuel economy (while generating less pollution) and sophisticated flight systems that allowed two pilots to safely operate even the largest and longest-range planes. Yield management systems allowed the airlines to minimize the number of empty seats on every flight, an essential goal when fares are low.

This period was a very tumultuous one for the airline industry as firms adjusted to the new reality of deregulation. Unfortunately, some major carriers simply could not adapt: Braniff failed in 1982, Western in 1986, Eastern and Pan Am in 1991.[23] Of the eight local service airlines that served various regional markets in 1978, only one, US Airways, survived into the 90s while Southwest was all that remained of the four intrastate airlines operating in California, Florida, and Texas. Most telling of all is that out of 119 airlines that started service between 1979 and 1998, 76 failed during the same period.[24] Some airlines simply went bankrupt while others were bought or merged with a larger carrier, but all disappeared one way or the other from the industry.

More Upheaval: 1999 to 2014

This period was very much defined by environmental events: September 11, 2001 and the use of commercial airliners as terrorist weapons; the ensuing war in the Mideast; rising fuel prices; and a global recession, just to name a few. When you add to this turmoil the rise of a new generation of "no-frills" competitors now known as low-cost carriers (LCCs), increasing global competition, declining revenues, and the continued contraction of the industry, the challenges become even more apparent.

9/11 and Its Aftermath

The attacks on the World Trade Center in New York forced airlines, passengers, and governments around the world to redefine their respective views of security. The United States immediately strengthened passenger screenings as did many other nations. The Transportation Security Administration (TSA) was established on November 19, 2001 and assumed responsibility for all civil aviation security functions from the FAA. In March 2003, TSA transferred from the Department of Transportation to the Department of Homeland Security, which was created in November 2002 to unify the nation's response to threats to the homeland.[25] The new procedures were more intrusive, restrictive, and time consuming, necessitating preplanning on the part of passengers to ensure they allowed sufficient time for the process. In other words, the days of dashing into the airport 30 minutes prior to departure and making the flight were gone forever. As time passed, procedures had to be modified as new threats arose and were handled. Items that used to be allowed in carry-on bags are now prohibited (nail files, pocket knives, and later on, liquids and gels over three ounces), adding to the confusion and processing time. Taken in sum, the impact on the passenger experience of heightened security, while necessary, was largely negative.

Fuel Costs

Fuel, which globally comprised 14 percent of a carrier's operating costs in 2003 when the average price per barrel of crude was $28.80, accounted for 30 percent 10 years later as the price per barrel rose to $108.[26] By the middle of 2013, oil prices began to fall and have continued to do so to the point that the airlines paid an average of $2.05 per gallon in June 2015.[27] The attendant reduction in operating costs from the streamlining of routes and the increased use of highly efficient aircraft means the cheaper fuel is even more impactful to the company's bottom line.[28]

Financial Recovery

Beginning in 2007, deteriorating consumer confidence and economic uncertainty due to the European debt crisis and the growing likelihood of a protracted period of slow growth in developed economies combined to plunge the world into a recession that persisted into 2011.[29] However, this situation exacerbated an already untenable situation. For most of the

2000s, U.S. passenger airlines were struggling to post operating profits. In 2008 alone, they lost $5.6 billion,[30] but things began to improve as operating profits rose to more than $5 billion in 2012[31] and almost $200 billion in 2013.[32] One reason credited for the industry's soaring profits is that carriers are not adding more capacity than demand can support. And to a large extent, they are trying to add capacity without adding airplanes by ensuring every flight is full.[33] In addition, companies are reaping billions by charging for everything from checking a bag to extra legroom. United, for instance, said that its revenue from such extra charges increased 16 percent in the third quarter, to more than $20 per passenger, compared with the same period in 2012.[34] Another factor is the wave of mergers that occurred among the nation's largest carriers at the turn of the decade: in 2008, Northwest Airlines merged with Delta,[35] while United and Continental did the same in 2010,[36] and American and US Airways in 2014.[37] This concentration of market power facilitated the stability necessary to implement many of the policies just discussed.

Low-Cost Carriers

The public interest in low-cost or low-service air transportation became a global phenomenon in the 2000s. Southwest, which started as an intra-Texas carrier in 1971, was the first of the second-generation LCCs in the United States, to be followed by others like JetBlue, Spirit, Allegiant, and a newer incarnation of Frontier. Similar airlines can be found in virtually every area of the world, all promoting lower cost flights and fewer (if any) free amenities than their full-service competition. Succeeding in this segment remains challenging, however, as profitability can remain just as elusive as it did for those firms following the same strategy in the 1980s.

Summary

This chapter has presented the high points of the industry's development from the beginnings of powered flight in 1904, through two world wars and a like number of major economic downturns, as well as other environmental events that have collectively shaped this global transportation system into the one we rely on today. In addition, the transition from economic regulation to deregulation completely transformed the way the airlines operated, and necessitated such a dramatic change in management skills that many carriers failed because their leaders could not make the transition to a free-market business model.

CHAPTER 2

The Global Airline Industry

Introduction

Airline operations differ from one part of the world to the other. First World, Second World, and Third World carriers will be discussed in order to understand how differences in management philosophy, cultural issues, and governmental influence affect carriers of different nationalities. The current business environment will then be examined as will the unpredictability of a global airline's operating environment. However, because the basic administrative structure within which all international air services operate has remained virtually unchanged since 1944, it will be presented first.

The Exchange of Air Rights Between Nations

Bilateral Agreements

In 1944, during the closing stages of World War II, 54 countries came together in Chicago, U.S., to discuss the future of international aviation. The conference resulted in the signing of the *Convention on International Civil Aviation*, commonly known as the Chicago Convention, which established the rules under which international aviation continues to operate. The treaty determined that no *scheduled* international air service may be operated over or into the territory of another state without its express permission and led to the development of a series of traffic rights that came to be known as the Five Freedoms (or Rights) of the Air that continue to form the basis of rights exchanged in air services negotiations today.[1] Briefly, these are:

> *First Freedom*—the right for an airline from one country to fly over another country without landing

Second Freedom—the right granted by one country to another country to land in its territory for nonrevenue purposes such as fuel or repairs (also referred to as a technical stop)

Third Freedom—the right for an airline to deliver revenue passengers from its home country to another country

Fourth Freedom—the right for an airline to deliver revenue passengers from another country to its home country

Fifth Freedom—the right for an airline to take passengers from its home country, deposit them at their destination in another country, then pick up additional passengers and take them on to additional international destinations[2]

Reflecting the massive changes that have occurred in the industry since these were promulgated, several other freedoms have since been added. Although most are not officially recognized under international treaties, they have been agreed to by a number of countries and are presented next.

Sixth Freedom—the right for an airline from Country A to carry passengers or cargo between Countries B and C via Country A

Seventh Freedom—the right for an airline to transport revenue passengers or cargo between two countries without transiting its own country

Eighth Freedom—the right for an airline from Country A to carry passengers or cargo between two points in Country B as long as the flight originates in Country A or a third Country C, also known as consecutive cabotage

Ninth Freedom—the right for an airline from one country to carry passengers or cargo within another country without restriction, otherwise known as pure cabotage[3]

The Office of International Aviation and the U.S. Department of State negotiate bilateral and multilateral air service agreements with the United States' foreign aviation partners. Such agreements provide the basis for airlines of the countries involved to provide international air services for passengers, cargo, and mail and are quite detailed, covering the following:

- **Traffic rights**—the routes airlines can fly, including cities that can be served within, between, and beyond the bilateral partners
- **Capacity**—the number of flights that can be operated or passengers that can be carried between the bilateral partners
- **Designation, ownership, and control**—the number of airlines the bilateral partners can nominate to operate services and the ownership criteria airlines must meet to be designated under the bilateral agreement. This clause sometimes includes foreign ownership restrictions
- **Tariffs**—that is prices. Some agreements require airlines to submit ticket prices to aeronautical authorities for approval
- Many other clauses addressing competition policy, safety, and security[4]

While the United States has advocated for a competitive free market in international aviation since 1944, the system is still overwhelmingly characterized by bilateral agreements negotiated between two countries. In fact, there are currently more than 3,000 of these agreements around the world, all of which are treaty-level documents agreed to by governments. Once signed, service rights are awarded to each nation's airlines by their respective governments consistent with the provisions agreed to in the bilateral. Naturally, as with any negotiation, the balance of power on each side may not be equal, which can lead a country to concede an air transport advantage in exchange for a gain in some other aspect of diplomacy totally unrelated to transportation. Not only are governments continually negotiating new treaties to allow international aviation to grow and to expand its carriers' access to new and emerging markets, but existing bilaterals have a finite life and must be renegotiated over time. Because the relative power of the participants may have changed dramatically over the years, the new agreement may be radically different than the old one. For example, the United States bilateral with Japan was first signed is 1952, and was not renegotiated until 1998.[5] Japan's growth from a destroyed nation after World War II to a global economic powerhouse placed it in a much stronger position and allowed it to negotiate a much more favorable agreement.

The United States strives to develop a competitive operating environment for U.S. airline services, but must work in a global environment that is not as supportive of free markets. Since 1992, the Department of Transportation has pursued an "open-skies" policy designed to eliminate government involvement in airline decision making about routes, capacity, and pricing in international markets. Open-skies agreements also contain provisions governing commercial opportunities, safety, and security. The United States has negotiated open-skies bilaterals with more than 100 countries that allow airlines from both nations to serve each other's markets without restrictions.[6]

Multilateral Agreements

In keeping with its commitment to free-market principles, the United States has negotiated two multilateral open-skies accords as well: (1) the 2001 Multilateral Agreement on the Liberalization of International Air Transportation (MALIAT) with New Zealand, Singapore, Brunei, and Chile, later joined by Samoa, Tonga, and Mongolia; and (2) the 2007 Air Transport Agreement with the European Community and its 27 Member States.[7] While the first agreement clearly favors the foreign countries, the precedent was set for subsequent negotiations like the second that embrace markets that are attractive for U.S. carriers.

Cabotage

But no matter how all-encompassing these agreements might be, the transport of domestic passengers (or freight) between points in their own country by a foreign carrier is rarely permitted. Thus, Lufthansa might have received Fifth Freedom Rights from the United States to carry passengers from Frankfurt on to Houston after dropping off other passengers from Germany in New York. But they cannot pick up new passengers in New York and take them to Houston. The principle of cabotage goes back hundreds of years to a time when nations were concerned about protecting domestic coastal shipping from foreign competition; as air transportation became more global, cabotage laws were applied to commercial aviation as well. In contrast, since 1997 the European Union (EU) has allowed all Community airlines unconditional access to all domestic EU markets, including routes considered cabotage.[8]

Global Airline Ownership and Operation

Though now outdated, looking at the world as comprised of first, second, and third world countries provides a useful framework for examining how governments utilize air transport to meet their national goals. For the purposes of this discussion, the following definitions will be used:

- The term "First World" refers to so-called developed, *capitalist*, industrial countries, roughly, a bloc of countries aligned with the United States after World War II, with more or less common political and economic interests: North America, Western Europe, Japan, and Australia.
- "Second World" refers to the former *communist–socialist*, industrial states (formerly the Eastern bloc, the territory and sphere of influence of the Union of Soviet Socialist Republics [USSR]) today: Russia, Eastern Europe (e.g., Poland) and some of the Turk States (e.g., Kazakhstan), as well as China.
- "Third World" embraces all the other countries, today often used to roughly describe the developing countries of Africa, Asia, and Latin America.[9]

First World Airlines

Most carriers based in these nations are either totally or primarily (less than 50 percent government ownership) private enterprises whose main objective is profitable operations. All operate western-made aircraft primarily manufactured by Boeing and Airbus industries staffed with well-qualified crews and maintained to the highest standards.

Second World Airlines

Prior to the breakup of the Soviet Union in 1990, all of the carriers in this category were government owned and operated utilizing only Russian-made aircraft. After the breakup, as much of the former Soviet bloc shifted more toward free enterprise, private airlines began to appear utilizing western as well as Russian-made aircraft. Typically, these for-profit operators must compete with a state-run flag carrier (e.g., Aeroflot or Air China), which can prove to be almost impossible.

Third World Airlines

The mix of companies here include some of the best and worst in the world, the former represented by Emirates (United Arab Emirates) and Qatar Airways (Qatar), the latter by a multitude of carriers in Africa where the vast majority of airlines banned from the EU are based.[10] Both the EU and the United States maintain "black lists" of carriers resulting from ground inspections that uncover badly maintained, dilapidated, or obsolete aircraft; an inability to correct faults that are identified; and the incapacity of the airline's home nation authority in charge of airline oversight and surveillance to ensure compliance with U.S. and EU regulations.[11]

Reasons for Operating an Airline

Airlines are in business for a variety of reasons including making a profit, projecting national prestige on a global stage, providing employment, and supporting national defense.

Profit

As noted earlier, profit is what drives most privately held carriers regardless of their location. Simply put, these companies must make money to survive; their interest in anything else, other than perhaps supporting the needs of national defense (recall the Civil Reserve Air Fleet [CRAF] in the United States), is a distant second.

Social Promotion

Virtually every country in the world has an international airline, including North Korea and Cuba. Clearly, profit is not the primary motivator for either of these nations' carriers. In fact, North Korea's Air Koryo received the only one-star rating among 190 airlines reviewed by the Skytrax service.[12] Sometimes, airlines provide a global presence for a country that may otherwise lack one. Alternatively, government-controlled airlines renowned for their high passenger service levels (e.g., Emirates and Singapore Airlines) use their reputation for excellence as an extension of the country itself. For those companies that must control costs and earn a profit, competing with carriers that do not worry about such things can be extremely difficult.

Xiamen Airlines is an interesting case in point. The Chinese carrier recently took delivery of the first of six Boeing 787s it has ordered to initiate flights between Xiamen (a city of almost 2 million people located on the southeast coast of China) and Amsterdam or Paris. As the remainder of their new aircraft arrive, the airline plans to start services to Australia and North America as well. The company initially expects to lose money on flying this airplane because it will be the first wide-body in the fleet and will be used to pioneer long routes. Moreover, the airline lacks brand recognition in the foreign markets that will be served, and although Xiamen is a well-developed city from which many tourists may wish to fly to Europe, it is not likely to strongly attract European travelers, especially those flying for business. So why operate such a service? According to Xiamen Airlines Deputy General Manager Zhao Chen:

> Our aim is not necessarily to make a profit with widebody aircraft. It is good enough not to lose money in operating them—or at least it would be consistent with our expectations if we operated the aircraft at a small loss. Xiamen Airlines' Boeing 787s will have a beneficial social and economic effect. Sometimes the aim of the airline industry is not to make money but, rather, to do good deeds.[13]

As a result, the city of Xiamen, which has an ownership share in the airline, will subsidize the losses as a cost of promoting the city and the region.[14]

Employment

Though not operated strictly for job creation purposes, transportation enterprises, particularly railroads and airlines, are often huge sources of employment especially when run by the state. For example, the Indian Railways is the largest employer in India and the eighth largest in the world.[15] Unfortunately, they, like their U.S. counterparts, also tend to be heavily unionized across all job categories, which makes privatization and the attendant need to achieve cost efficiency through labor reductions absolutely essential and extremely difficult. Absent those changes, the state must either continue to support the company or let it fail and deal with the consequences as Belgium did in 2001 when its state airline Sabena went bankrupt taking as many as 14,000 jobs with it.[16] Indeed, employment issues continue to challenge managers as the industry becomes more competitive. Despite intense pressure from the French government to avoid layoffs, Air France–KLM has moved ahead with plans to slash more than 5,100 jobs at its Air France unit by the end of 2013—just over 10 percent of its workforce of 49,000. Another 1,300 jobs are being eliminated at its smaller KLM unit. These reductions follow on the heels of staff cuts earlier in 2012 that resulted from early retirements and other voluntary departures.[17]

National Defense Needs

From the earliest days of commercial aviation, the United States has advocated a partnership between its airlines and the military. Each major piece of legislation discussed in Chapter 1 has included a statement of national policy supporting the development of an air transportation system able to meet the needs of the foreign and domestic commerce of the United States, of the Postal Service, and of the national defense.[18] The voluntary partnership embodied in the CRAF has helped fulfill this requirement since its inception, reducing the need for military assets while providing revenue to the carriers. Nations that operate their own airlines can certainly draft them into military service, although their armed forces tend to perform those tasks themselves. In fact, some third-world countries like Sir Lanka even utilize their Air Force to provide commercial services.[19]

Current Situation

Privatization

For many nations today, operating a global airline has become too expensive given all of the competing societal demands for scarce resources. While some countries such as China continue to sustain large government-owned carriers, others are choosing to attempt privatization by offering them for sale to commercial interests. Simply put, privatization is the process of converting a publicly operated enterprise into a privately owned and operated entity. Many countries around the world have privatized formerly state-run enterprises such as banks, airlines, steel companies, utilities, phone systems, and large manufacturers. A wave of privatization swept through Russia and Eastern Europe after the fall of Communism in the 1990s, and through some Latin American countries such as Peru, as new democratic governments were established. When a company is privatized, shares formerly owned by the government, as well as management control, are offered to the commercial sector. The theory behind privatization is that these enterprises run far more efficiently and offer better service to customers when owned by stockholders instead of the government.[20] Unfortunately, making a previously state-run carrier attractive to private investors can involve huge changes in labor and business practices that may prove so unpopular that implementation is simply impossible. The only recourse then is to continue government support to some degree or, as in the case of Belgium, allow the airline to fail.

An interesting wrinkle is that a prospective investor could be from another country which is why governments such as the EU and the United States limit foreign investment in their respective airlines to 49 percent and 25 percent, respectively.[21] United Arab Emirates-based Etihad Airways wants to acquire 49 percent ownership of Italy's Alitalia. The Italian government, which is not a direct shareholder in the company but still has strong influence, is willing to accept unheard-of concessions and cutbacks just to keep the airline out of their hands.[22] Because foreign investment is viewed as preferable to the failure to an airline, both the United States and the EU are evaluating whether or not to raise or even eliminate the current limit. However, issues relating to national defense and the CRAF make the issue much more problematic in America than in Europe.

Strategic Alliances

Airlines often form voluntary alliances with each other as a way to offer services to destinations they do not serve directly via rights awarded from the bilateral process. These began quite simply, with one agreeing to award its frequent flier miles for travel on the other, but have since grown into globe-spanning networks of multiple carriers each honoring the tickets and frequent traveler awards of the other. The largest of these is the Star Alliance made up of 27 airlines from around the world,[23] followed by Sky Team with 20 members,[24] and OneWorld comprised of 16 carriers.[25] Through a practice known as code sharing, airlines are effectively able to extend their route structures by writing and selling tickets to destinations served by a partner. They may also share gates and ground support duties at some airports, thereby reducing costs. Code sharing also allows alliance members to effectively share aircraft by commingling ticket holders from one or more partners onto a single plane. Passengers gain from the expanded service offerings, the retention of their frequent flier benefits when changing airlines, one-stop baggage checking from origin to final destination, and more convenient connections.

Disadvantages to passengers are minor. Some may be unaware their trip will be at least partially on a foreign carrier. For example, Delta Airlines offers a flight from Charleston, South Carolina to Seoul, South Korea where the only leg actually flown by Delta is the one between Charleston and Atlanta; the remainder is via Korean Airlines.[26]

Unfortunately, service levels can vary across airlines, so a company must make every attempt to select partners who share their operating standards and commitment to customer satisfaction. Delta has been known to drop airlines from Sky Team when their standards fall, because passengers tend to blame Delta for their unsatisfactory experience even though they were on another carrier. A more significant problem can arise in the event of an accident. When Swissair Flight 111 crashed off the coast of Nova Scotia in 1998, 53 of the passengers lost were on Delta tickets.[27] As a result, Delta found itself a defendant in a number of lawsuits alleging that, because the airline had issued the ticket, it was responsible for the passengers' safety.[28] Similarly, recovering damages in the event of a partner carrier accident can be very difficult, especially if that airline is owned by a foreign government.

Low-Cost Carriers

Once referred to as no-frills airlines, these companies focus on offering extremely low fares with concomitant levels of service. While not new in the United States (People Express, Southwest, JetBlue, Spirit Air, and Allegiant Air) or Europe (Laker, EasyJet, and Ryanair), they have proliferated across Asia and Australia as well. Interestingly, the major U.S. airlines initially either ignored these upstarts or reacted by setting up low-cost subsidiaries (Delta's Song and United's Ted) to compete with them.[29] Unfortunately, failing to take this new business model seriously allowed Southwest and JetBlue, for example, to gain competitive advantages they hold to this day. Song and Ted, on the other hand, lasted only three and five years, respectively, both proving to be short-lived and costly failures.[30] In Europe, a similar pattern emerged during the same period, as upstarts Ryanair and EasyJet grew to become the largest low-cost carriers (LCCs) on the continent, while more established airlines like Lufthansa and British Airways failed to unseat them with their own budget-minded sub-brands. Air France–KLM and Lufthansa are both trying again, but they may simply be too late to the market now.[31] Even Air Canada, which has long dominated the Canadian market, was unable to keep its LCC Tango alive for more than three years. In each of these cases, a better-funded competitor, backed by an experienced player in the market, lost out to a younger, smaller company, despite a nearly identical offering and pricing structure.[32] Even the established airlines in Asia are realizing these competitors are here to stay. There are currently 47 LCCs operating in the Asia Pacific region, including 23 in Southeast Asia, 16 in North Asia, six in South Asia, and two in Australia. These 47 carriers ended 2013 with a combined in-service fleet of 992 aircraft, according to the CAPA Fleet Database. Indonesia's Lion Air is the largest single LCC, with a fleet of 94 in-service aircraft, according to the CAPA Fleet Database. But Malaysia's AirAsia is still the continent's largest LCC group, with an in-service fleet as of December 31, 2013 of 172 aircraft compared to 133 for the Lion Group.[33]

While mostly regional, long-haul LCCs are starting to emerge as well. There is particular interest in the South East Asia–Australia trade where estimates say as many as 10 are planning to go head-to-head with established airlines like Qantas, Singapore, and Cathay Pacific.[34] The list includes not only Lion Air and AirAsia, but Cebu Pacific from the Philippines, Citilink and Batik Air also from Indonesia, Vietnam's VietJet Air, Jin Air from Korea, Thai joint venture NokScoot, Malaysia's Malindo, and AirAsia X franchises in Thailand and Indonesia.[35] Whether or not these companies actually start their services, let alone succeed, remains to be seen. But the interest in this business model is no longer confined to Asia. In fact, Norwegian Air Shuttle has applied to offer similar services between the United States and Europe via Ireland, but is encountering opposition both from U.S. airlines and the government.[36] The topic of what constitutes a successful LCC business model will be explored more fully in a subsequent chapter.

Deregulation

Many nations around the world have followed the lead of the United States by freeing their airlines from economic regulation. The United States made the change in 1978 and was virtually alone in allowing market forces to allocate air transport services rather than government mandates. Since then, nations as diverse as India, Canada, Russia, and Australia, just to name a few, have followed suit. However, all of these actions apply to domestic services only. International air transport is still based on the bilateral structure previously discussed. A more significant development has been the growth of multinational trade organizations formed to advance the collective power of their member states. The best known example is the EU, which, while emphasizing deregulation within the Union, had allowed the individual countries to continue negotiating their own bilaterals. However, the European Court ruled in 2002 that such arrangements unfairly discriminated against those members who lacked similar agreements. As a result, the EU has started to negotiate open-skies air service agreements with non-EU countries on behalf of its member nations, and has done so with Australia and New Zealand. Negotiators are working on similar arrangements with China and the

United States, which could make cabotage in both of those markets a contentious issue in the future.

Discriminatory Airport Charges

Airlines transporting passengers and freight pay fees for the use of airport facilities. These may include charges related to aircraft landings, the processing of passengers and freight, and the use of airport infrastructure. Of course, these charges are ultimately paid, indirectly, by passengers and shippers via the ticket price or freight forwarding fees. Charges are applied in different ways, depending on the service that they cover. Passenger charges are levied per passenger while other charges are applied per aircraft landing or takeoff. Airport charging systems are in many instances imposed and governed by the national authorities. Even where the airports concerned are privately owned, the charges have to comply with regulatory parameters set by the authorities. Charging systems can also work as management tools. By varying certain charges, airports can try to increase the use of airport infrastructure or reduce the environmental impact of aviation.[37] The challenge is to ensure these are imposed in a nondiscriminatory way that does not favor one carrier over another. For example, Italy has a two-tiered system that charges lower landing and takeoff fees for intra-EU flights, while fees for extra-EU flights (those going to or from Italy via a foreign location like the United States) are much higher.[38]

Unforeseen Events

Airlines providing international services may often find themselves facing unexpected and deadly environmental risks from a variety of sources.

Military Strife

The unfortunate loss of Malaysian Airlines Flight 17 over Eastern Ukraine in July 2014 sadly highlighted the vulnerability of the world's air carriers to the sophistication of today's weapons systems regardless of where they are being used. In fact, since 1973, five passenger planes (not including

Flight 17) have been shot down by military aircraft, including the 1988 loss of Iran Air Flight 655 to a missile fired by the USS Vincennes who mistook it for an Iranian fighter.[39] Ongoing instability in the Middle East continues to disrupt commercial traffic into and out of the region, with the ever-present risk of more severe consequences to the carriers serving the area.

Disease

The airline industry was battered more than a decade ago by the outbreak of SARS, or severe acute respiratory syndrome, which was mainly transmitted through respiratory droplets produced when infected people coughed or sneezed. The outbreak, which originated in China in late 2002, infected about 8,400 people worldwide and killed 900, according to World Health Organization estimates. The SARS outbreak devastated the travel and tourism industry, with as much as two-thirds of the normal passenger volume for Asian carriers evaporating during the outbreak's peak. Some cases jumped to Canada as well. Hotel occupancy rates plummeted in places such as Singapore and Hong Kong, retail sales fell, and airlines canceled large numbers of flights. As a result of the 2014 outbreak of the Ebola virus in West Africa, several European carriers curtailed services to the region as have some large African carriers. Only two U.S. airlines, Delta and United, serve Africa at all, both with very limited coverage. That said, Delta dropped a connecting flight between Accra, Ghana and Monrovia, the capitol of Liberia, in August 2014.[40] Despite the low number of flights and assurances that the disease does not spread via airborne particles, fears about the virus caused airline shares (and other travel stocks) to fall in October.[41]

Natural Disasters

The 2010 eruption of the Eyjafjallajökull volcano in Iceland shut down air travel over parts of Europe for almost a month. In some cases, airline disruptions due to volcanic activity can last much longer. It is not visibility that worries pilots when ash clouds fill the air, but the airborne chemicals that can damage the engines, clog ventilation, and cause the aircraft to stall.[42] In fact, in 1989, all four engines of a KLM Boeing 747 flying from Amsterdam to Tokyo temporarily shut down when the plane flew through a cloud of ash from the erupting Redoubt Volcano in Alaska. The aircraft descended from 25,000 feet to 12,000 feet in eight minutes before the crew was able to restart two of the engines, and all four were operating when the plane landed in Anchorage, where it had been scheduled to stop for refueling.[43] Because of the danger to air travel posed by an eruption, the Icelandic Meteorological Office is actively watching the Bardarbunga volcano because of its increased seismic activity.[44] Similarly, the 2010 earthquake in Haiti and 2014's Hurricane Odile in Mexico's Baja California damaged local airports so badly that even emergency air services could not be provided until a basic clean-up had been accomplished.[45]

Political Situations

National politics can often adversely impact a carrier's operations. One of the most significant events of the 20th century was the breakup of the USSR in 1991. The state-run carriers operated by the former Republics were immediately thrown into a competitive marketplace they were ill-equipped to deal with. In many cases, entrepreneurs stepped in to start private airlines with varying degrees of success. Aeroflot began service in 1923 as the Soviet state-run airline and is now a semiprivate company providing both domestic and international services from Moscow.[46] Furthermore, the disintegration of the Soviet military made a flood of cheap surplus military transport aircraft available for sale to anyone who wanted one regardless of their intentions.

In a more recent case, international airlines serving Venezuela cut their service in half between January 2014 and August 2014, or canceled it all together because the government continued to hold back on releasing $3.8 billion in airline ticket revenue due to strict currency controls.[47] Myanmar's efforts to expand its airline industry have been hampered by the fact that many of the country's airlines are owned or backed by people on a U.S. government sanctions list. Investors use the list as a guide on ties to avoid in Myanmar because they fear the reputational risk and compliance issues that might arise for them or their business units in the United States.[48] Finally, changes within the carrier's home country can also impact its operations. Qantas Airways had a net loss of AUD 2.84 billion in their last fiscal year, which was partially due to softening demand for domestic travel. In addition, a drop in the Australian dollar to below parity against its U.S. counterpart increased its jet fuel costs that are paid in U.S. dollars.[49]

Chapter Summary

This chapter examines the genesis of today's international aviation arena including how air services are exchanged between nations and how different countries view their global airline services. The current business operating environment was discussed as was the impact of unforeseen events on a global air carrier.

CHAPTER 3

Industry Organization

Introduction

In the United States, anyone who wants to provide air transportation service as an air carrier must first obtain two separate authorizations from the Department of Transportation (DOT):

- Economic authority from the Office of the Secretary in the form of a certificate for interstate or foreign passenger and cargo authority
- Safety authority in the form of an Air Carrier Certificate and Operations Specifications from the Federal Aviation Administration (FAA)

Economic authority for U.S. carriers may be in the form of a certificate for interstate or foreign passengers and cargo and mail authority, a certificate for interstate or foreign all-cargo authority, or authorization as a commuter air carrier. As of May 29, 2015, there were 114 certificated U.S. Air Carriers.[1]

In the broadest sense, all carriers are either for-hire or not-for-hire; that is, they either offer services to the general public or they do not. For-hire carriers are passenger and cargo airlines providing scheduled services over fixed routes, charter companies performing long-term contract work, and firms that provide ad-hoc services moving people or project cargo on demand. The operation of aircraft that are not-for-hire is also referred to as private transportation; that is, nontransportation firms operating their own aircraft to move their own products or people. These do not require economic authority, but must comply with all FAA requirements for safe aircraft operation. Each type of air transport will be discussed in detail in the following sections.

For-Hire Carriers

Introduction

For-hire carriers are airlines with which the public is most familiar. In fact, most of the material discussed in the earlier chapters pertains to this sector of the industry. Collectively referred to as common carriers, they offer their services to the general public for compensation. To ensure all customers are treated equally, governments generally take some degree of interest in the carriers' operation either by actively regulating them or by monitoring their activities within the context of a free market, as the United States has done since 1978. As a result, the DOT uses a straightforward four-part test to determine the economic fitness of a new applicant:

- It examines the managerial competence of key personnel to determine whether they have sufficient business and aviation experience to operate an airline, and whether the management team, as a whole, possesses the background and experience necessary for the specific kind of operations proposed.
- It reviews the operating and financial plans to see whether the applicant has a reasonable understanding of the costs of starting its operations and either has on hand, or has a specific and verifiable plan for raising, the necessary capital to commence operations. Before being granted effective air carrier authority, the applicant must submit third-party verification that it has acquired the necessary capital to conduct its operations.
- It looks at the applicant's compliance record to see whether it and its owners and managers have a history of safety violations or consumer fraud activities that would pose a risk to the traveling public, or whether other factors indicate that the applicant or its key personnel are unlikely to comply with government laws, rules, and directives.
- The applicant must establish that it is owned and controlled by U.S. citizens.[2]

In other words, all the DOT cares about is that the applicant is controlled by U.S. citizens who have the managerial and financial skills to run the business and have not done anything illegal. Awarding the certificate only allows the applicant to enter the competitive fray; whether or not the new carrier succeeds is totally up to management and, arguably, of little concern to the government.

Scheduled Passenger Airlines

Scheduled passenger airlines are some of the oldest continuously operating airlines in the world, a group collectively referred to as legacy carriers, along with numerous competitors who have entered the market in recent years. Regardless of longevity, they share, to at least some degree, the following traits, all of which generate costs:

- The operation of relatively large aircraft that must be fueled and maintained
- The requirement for airport space to handle passenger check-in and loading or unloading
- Support services such as baggage handling, catering, and aircraft ground support
- The need for elaborate reservation systems
- Large expenditures for advertising and promotion

As competition has become more acute, companies have been struggling to reduce these expenses by reducing onboard services and staffing, managing fares to ensure all flights are as full as possible, and operating fuel-efficient aircraft. In addition, carriers now charge extra fees for value-added services that were, at one time, free: booking a reservation over the phone, changing a flight, checking a bag, and in-flight entertainment, just to name a few. In fact, in 2014, U.S. airlines earned $3.5 billion from luggage fees alone and are expected to record a total net profit of $13.2 billion in 2015.[3] Despite this good news, competitive pressures continue, especially from overseas. As an example, Norwegian Air International (NAI) has applied to the DOT for a foreign air carrier permit to fly to the United States. NAI is a Norwegian-owned low-cost carrier (LCC) that holds an air carrier certification from Ireland, but does not fly to or from Ireland. Furthermore, the company does not use Norwegian or even Irish flight crews, but rather Bangkok-based crews hired through a Singapore employment agency who work under Singapore Labor Law. This "nation-shopping" model has enabled NAI to artificially lower operating costs by suppressing collective bargaining rights and substantially lowering the wages, benefits, and conditions offered to these rented workers as compared to their Norwegian-based counterparts. This structure is similar to the "flag of convenience" model common in the maritime industry that allows ships to be registered in whatever nation has the lowest fees and without regard for the country of ownership. For example, Mediterranean Shipping Company, the world's second largest container shipping line, is owned by an Italian company headquartered in Geneva with ships registered in countries all over the world. The issue is that the vessel is considered, for legal purposes, to be the soil of the country in which it is flagged and subject to its laws instead of presumably more rigorous requirements in the firm's home nation.[4] Needless to say, the four largest American carriers vigorously oppose the award of a certificate to NAI, as do related labor unions and legal experts. The top 10 scheduled passenger airlines in the world based on passenger–kilometers flown (one passenger flown one kilometer) are shown in Table 3.1.

Scheduled Cargo Airlines

For years, some of the major U.S. airlines also operated dedicated cargo aircraft in support of scheduled freight services run alongside their passenger operations. Though still common overseas, no U.S. passenger carrier maintains freighters today, although a great deal of cargo does move in the belly of passenger flights. The top 10 airlines in 2013 based on scheduled freight ton–kilometers flown (one ton moved one kilometer) are shown in Table 3.2.

Note that 7 out of the 10 on the list transport passengers as well.

Nonscheduled Firms

Charter Companies

Chartered flights are similar to charter buses in that they are often reserved by groups for their express use. When taking a tour of Europe,

Table 3.1 Total international and domestic scheduled passenger–kilometers flown in 2013

Rank	Airline	Passenger–kilometers (millions)
1	United Airlines	286,802
2	Delta Air Lines	277,560
3	Emirates	209,377
4	American Airlines	206,551
5	China Southern Airlines	147,841
6	Southwest Airlines	145,124
7	Lufthansa	144,236
8	Air France	136,405
9	British Airways	130,129
10	Qantas Airways	110,203

Source: https://www.iata.org/publications/Pages/wats-freight-km.aspx (accessed June 10, 2015).

Table 3.2 Total international and domestic scheduled freight ton–kilometers flown in 2013

Rank	Airline	Freight ton–kilometers (millions)
1	FedEx (cargo only)	16,127
2	UPS Airlines (cargo only)	10,584
3	Emirates	10,459
4	Cathay Pacific Airways	8,241
5	Korean Air Lines	7,666
6	Lufthansa	7,218
7	Singapore Airlines	6,240
8	Cargolux (cargo only)	5,225
9	Qatar Airways	4,972
10	China Airlines	4,813

Source: https://www.iata.org/publications/Pages/wats-freight-km.aspx (accessed June 10, 2015).

the group tour bus ferries everyone from site to site and city to city. This bus is reserved for the group; it's not a municipal transit bus making a set route of stops or a Greyhound long-distance bus open to any passengers (both of these are examples of for-hire transportation). The tour company has reserved the bus for a specific purpose. The same model is found in air transportation, although, in practice, many charter airlines do essentially follow a set schedule, with a certain number of flights per week to desirable tourist destinations. Even in this case, individual passengers do not book tickets for the flight; they are sold in bulk to a tour company or travel agency. Similarly, a company may decide to book a trip for some reason—to transport the entire organization on a company vacation, for instance—that has unique scheduling requirements. Charter flights can fly into smaller regional airports that are off-limits to major commercial airlines or served infrequently. Charter flights are particularly useful for reaching destinations with limited commercial flight service that would require passengers to make multiple connections. Furthermore, chartered flights fall into the category of general aviation, a distinction that exempts passengers from some of the regulations associated with commercial flights.[5]

The demand for such specific services can be huge. The aforementioned example discusses the leisure travel industry, but sports teams, musical acts, touring theatrical productions, and religious groups are also potential customers who would typically enter into a contract with the carrier to provide services over some period of time. The downside for passengers is that the airline may not be one with which they are familiar. While not a grave concern in the United States or Europe, for example, there are some parts of the world where it could be. One of the biggest demands for charter passenger services occurs each year when Muslim pilgrims perform the Hajj. Faithful from all over the world make the annual round-trip to Mecca for five days to pray as one community, celebrating their history and giving thanks for blessings. In 2012, almost 3.2 million people went on Hajj, with 1.7 million of them coming from outside of Saudi Arabia.[6] In 2014, 14,500 went from China alone on 94 chartered flights.[7] At least one airline, PT Garuda Indonesia, flag carrier of the world's largest Islamic country, has expressed interest in a "Hajj-friendly" Airbus A380 that could theoretically be configured to carry 850 people.[8] These passengers can be very challenging because many do not speak English (or anything but their local language), have never flown before, and are generally unsophisticated travelers. Another large user of charter services is the U.S. Department of Defense (DOD), which awarded $545 million in Airlift Services Contracts to various U.S. carriers encompassing both passengers and freight for the period October 2014 to September 2015.[9] Recall that the DOD allocates this business to the airlines in exchange for their participation in the Civil Reserve Air Fleet (CRAF). Because of the lucrative nature of the charter business in general, many scheduled airlines participate in it as well, maintaining divisions dedicated to meeting specific needs not supportable with their normal operations.

Project or Ad-Hoc Carriers

Project or ad hoc airlines provide on-demand, point-to-point services for cargo that is unconventional in some way (size, shape, value), moves under unusual circumstances, or requires special handling not available via any other mode of transportation. Typically, these services compete with ocean shipping as the only realistic alternative for moving this type of freight internationally. An excellent example of such a company is Antonov Airlines, a Ukrainian carrier that has been very successful at exploiting the niche market of airlifting large-size and super-heavy cargoes to 800 airports around the world, utilizing a fleet that includes one AN-225 (a one-of-a-kind behemoth with six engines) and seven AN-124 wide-body freighters (similar in size and appearance to a USAF C-5) along with several smaller aircraft. For example, their work has included the delivery of a 175-ton transformer from Linz, Austria, to Houston, Texas; a 186.7 ton generator from Frankfurt, Germany, to Yerevan, Armenia; and 247 tons of large-size construction equipment from Prague, Czech Republic, to Tashkent, Uzbekistan. Often these loads necessitate the development of special preparation and loading technologies that challenge the aircraft's structural and performance capabilities.[10] What makes these aircraft so attractive is that they offer drive-on and drive-off capability that no other civilian wide-body aircraft can match. The freight moved could simply not be handled by any other airline.

When the U.S. DOD began building Mine-Resistant Ambush Protected (MRAP) vehicles in 2007, the military wanted to move them to the troops in the Middle East as quickly as possible. Utilizing sealift cost $13,000 per vehicle, but took 3 to 4 weeks in transit time. By air, using USAF C-17s, the cost was roughly $150,000 each, but the equipment arrived in a matter of days. Unfortunately, a C-17 can only carry three

MRAPs because each weighs approximately 38,000 pounds; therefore, the military contracted with two Ukrainian carriers (Volga-Dnepr and Polet Cargo Airlines) to assist using AN-124s, which can each accommodate up to six of the units.[11] As a result, between 2007 and 2012, aircraft belonging to airlines based in a nation that once was a part of the Soviet Union became a common sight at Charleston Air Force Base, South Carolina.[12]

Project carriers also have some unique operating characteristics. First, almost all their flights are one-way; that is, they depart from City A with a load destined for City B. From City B, they transit empty (unless they are fortunate enough to have a load in City B) to City C where they pick up cargo destined for City D. Another transit leg follows to City E and so on. Given that home base may be City X in this example, the crew and aircraft can be away for long periods of time. During those stops, the airplane serves as the accommodation for at least some of the crew, and trip-related purchases even for large expenses like fuel may require cash. Second, pricing for such specialized moves is very inelastic; that is, the carrier can charge whatever the customer is willing to pay because both know the buyer has essentially no alternative for moving its cargo. However, the airline must ensure that all related costs required for the move are known and factored into its quote. For example, empty transit flights, the need for specialized loading or unloading equipment, and airport fees must be anticipated. In one case many years ago, a now defunct U.S. airline was bidding to transport specialized oil drilling equipment into Saudi Arabia with a B747. The job required that several pieces of custom equipment be designed to get the cargo on and off the aircraft; hence, the company's bid was extremely high. Despite management's view that the bid was noncompetitive, the firm actually won the contract. They built the required equipment, transported it to Saudi Arabia with the cargo, and simply abandoned it there after they unloaded.

Other Carriers

Some firms focus on niche markets like medical transport, sightseeing, and air taxi services, all of which involve carrying paying passengers and therefore come under the purview of federal guidelines. One unique specialized U.S. carrier was Air America, an airline secretly owned by the Central Intelligence Agency (CIA), which was a vital component in the agency's operations in Laos from 1955 until the war's end in 1975. By the summer of 1970, the airline had some two dozen twin-engine transports, several larger planes including a Boeing 727, another two dozen short-takeoff-and-landing (STOL) aircraft, and 30 helicopters dedicated to operations in Laos. There were more than 300 pilots, copilots, flight mechanics, and air freight specialists flying out of Laos and Udorn, Thailand. During 1970, Air America airdropped or landed 46 million pounds of foodstuffs—mainly rice—in Laos. Helicopter flight time reached more than 4,000 hours a month in the same year. Air America crews transported tens of thousands of troops and refugees, flew emergency medevac missions and rescued downed airmen throughout Laos, inserted and extracted road-watch teams, flew nighttime airdrop mission over the Ho Chi Minh trail, and monitored sensors along infiltration routes. In addition, the company conducted a highly successful photo reconnaissance program, and engaged in numerous clandestine missions using night vision glasses and state-of-the-art electronic equipment. Without Air America's presence, the CIA's effort in Laos could not have been sustained. Unfortunately, the airline's reputation was tarnished by allegations of organized profiteering from drug smuggling that, while never proven, continue to this day.[13]

Clandestine Transportation

There has always been a demand for illicit cross-border transport services for people and goods. Unscrupulous operators undoubtedly exist in all modes, but the focus here is on air transportation. In fact, even first-world countries like the United States host their share of small questionable airlines. The problem became global when the fall of the Soviet Union in 1991 suddenly made large numbers of military cargo aircraft and crews idle. The planes were cheap to obtain on the open market and the personnel trained to operate them were desperate for work; therefore, many ad-hoc charter airlines began operating in the former republics. By and large, they offer their services to whomever is willing to pay with little regard for what they are transporting and where they are going.

International trafficking networks make extensive use of these resources. The planes are notorious for being underserviced and in violation of safety standards and are in fact often banned from serving EU and U.S. markets. The pilots, often without work for months, are willing to fly unsafe aircraft to obscure destinations and to look the other way on the cargo. The people behind the networks are rarely identified. In December 2009, Air West, based in the Republic of Georgia, flew an Ilyushin IL-76 (a USAF C-141 lookalike) from Ukraine to Pyongyang. After picking up cargo in North Korea, the aircraft flew to Bangkok where it stopped to refuel and was detained by Thai authorities. A search of the plane's cargo, after a tip-off from U.S. intelligence sources, revealed 35 tons of crated weapons inside the fuselage. The load included large numbers of rocket-propelled grenades (RPGs), man-portable surface-to-air missiles, and two mobile multiple-rocket launchers. The crew, who said they believed they were carrying heavy equipment for oil operations, were all men in their 50s and former members of the Soviet Air Force.

The IL-76 was designed to carry heavy machinery to remote areas of Russia. Its ability to land on rough airstrips in remote regions makes it an ideal aircraft for transporting illicit cargoes. The aircraft stopped in Thailand allegedly has a long involvement in transporting shady cargos. According to sources in the airfreight business, planes frequently change hands and registration numbers. The IL-76 detained in Bangkok was previously owned by a private Kazakh company, East Wing, then bought by another Kazakh airline, Beibers, which in turn sold it on to Air West. For this flight, the plane was leased out to SP Transport Limited, a Ukrainian company. Security analysts and freight operators say this type of paper trail is par for the course. Companies are shut down after being identified as trafficking in weapons or other illicit items or violating air safety regulations, only to reopen under different names. Aircraft similarly change registration or are sold or leased to other freight companies to disguise their business. The facilitators and buyers of this shipment so far remain a mystery. The winding paper trail and fly-by-night companies involved make shipments such as these difficult to trace. Initial speculation was that the shipment was destined for Sri Lanka, Pakistan, or the Middle East, but the crew never admitted to knowing where the shipment was ultimately going and were eventually sent home. Sadly, the demand for such services by North Korea, Iran, and many nations in Africa ensures their continued, even if unsafe, operation.[14]

Not-for-Hire (Private) Carriers

As mentioned in this chapter's introduction, private carriers are nontransportation companies that use their own vehicles (trucks, aircraft, ships, etc.) to move their own products. They do not offer their services to the general public for compensation. Most private transport of goods is found in the motor carrier industry, while similar movement of people is primarily found in air transportation.

Cargo

Regardless of mode, there are a number of reasons a company may elect to handle their own transportation rather than utilizing a for-hire firm: the need for specialized equipment, the desire for more control over the move, tight scheduling, or because management thinks it's cheaper. Boeing, as an example, operates a fleet of four B747 freighters (known as Dreamlifters), each highly modified with a raised fuselage and a swing-open tail that allow for the movement of large aircraft components from vendors located all over the world into assembly plants in Everett, Washington, and Charleston, South Carolina. Similarly, Airbus relies on a fleet of five A300-600STs (nicknamed Belugas), each with an additional wider fuselage section and a lowered cockpit to allow cargo loading through the front of the aircraft. This fleet makes more than 60 flights each week, carrying parts for all of Airbus' planes from manufacturing sites—for example, wings in the UK, tails in Spain—to the final assembly facilities in either Toulouse, Hamburg, or Tianjin. In fact, an even larger version is planned to enter service in 2020.[15]

Passenger

Many companies maintain fleets of aircraft to move their employees between corporate locations for the same reasons identified previously: better service than is commercially available, unique scheduling requirements, and so on. For example, Kimberly–Clark Corporation began providing air transportation for company executives and engineers between the company's Neenah, Wisconsin headquarters and their mills. Early employee shuttle destinations included Chicago O'Hare, Memphis, and Atlanta's Fulton County Airport. In 1984, the company actually used their private operation to form Midwest Express, a scheduled passenger airline that flew until 2009 when it was acquired by Republic Airways and ceased operations as an independent company.[16]

Companies such as NetJets offer fractional aircraft ownership whereby customers purchase an interest in a specific serial-numbered aircraft from the firm's fleet, which guarantees them aircraft availability with as little as four to six hours' notice. Because they actually own a part of the plane, buyers receive the financial benefits of a capital equipment acquisition along with predictable costs that include the following:

- One-time acquisition fee—based on share size and aircraft type
- Monthly management fee—covers indirect operating costs such as pilot salaries, training, hangar use, liability insurance, and owner services support
- Occupied hourly fee—covers direct operating costs such as maintenance, landing fees, and standard fuel for each specific flight
- Other fees—include hourly fuel fee, fuel tax surcharge, Federal Excise Tax (if applicable), international fees (as applicable), and ground transportation, if requested[17]

The biggest upfront cost is a one-time acquisition fee: For the Phenom 300 Platinum Edition jet, the second smallest in the fleet, a 1/16 interest, or 50 flight hours, costs $550,000. The largest share possible is a one-half interest, or 400 hours of flight time, which costs $4.4 million. For that same jet, the monthly management fee for a 50-hour share is $9,600, while a 400-hour share costs $60,000. The occupied fee is the same regardless of jet size, at $1,950 per hour. Owners sign up for a two-year, two-and-a-half-year, or three-year commitment, depending on the size of the aircraft, and NetJets has a guaranteed buy-back option after that commitment is up.[18] Again, because the passengers are considered owners, the company is not engaged in for-hire transportation.

Commercial Aircraft Manufacturing

The fortunes of the world's air carriers and the manufacturers of the aircraft they depend on are inextricably intertwined. Boeing and Airbus Industries are the primary suppliers of airliners, although competition from producers in Russia, China, and Canada for smaller, high-volume aircraft is increasing.[19] Forecasts for growth in new markets through 2023 drastically alter today's world mapping of commercial aviation—not only in sheer air traffic demand, but also the geographies where fleets will be needed to satisfy that demand. In fact, Boeing predicts the world will see demand for 35,280 new jet aircraft from now through 2032 at a value of $4.8 trillion, with single-aisle aircraft accounting for most of that demand.[20]

Despite the huge upside, aircraft manufacturing is an incredibly risky business. Designing a new airplane from scratch can result in the manufacturer incurring billions of dollars in cost before the first aircraft is delivered, which effectively results in them betting the company on the success of the endeavor.[21] Pricing is especially problematic because aircraft manufacturing is a classic example of an industry that exemplifies learning curve theory. As shown in Figure 3.1, the premise is that repetition of the same operation results in less time or effort expended

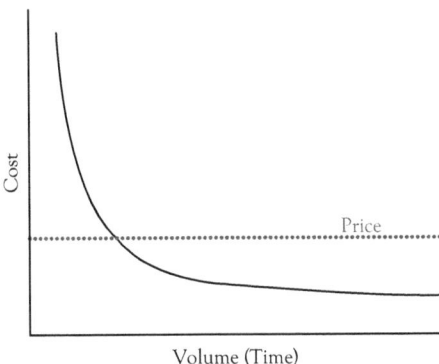

Figure 3.1 Manufacturing learning curve

on that operation over time. For example, the direct labor man-hours necessary to complete a unit of production will decrease by a constant percentage each time the production quantity is doubled. If the rate of improvement is 20 percent between doubled quantities, then the learning percent would be 80 percent.[22] While the learning curve emphasizes time, the application of cost is easily done. Note that a certain number of units must be produced before the learning curve is even reached. Thus, the costs associated with the earliest aircraft (in this example) are so high that no carrier would pay a price sufficient to cover them. Rather, the manufacturer must set a price based upon production levels that may not occur for years or, in the worst case, never. In order to mitigate that risk, the producer always seeks an airline to be the launch customer who commits to buy a certain number of the planes essentially sight unseen. Pan Am often served this role for Boeing with the B707 in the 1950s and the B747 ten years later, while All Nippon Airways did the same for the B787 and Singapore Airlines for the Airbus A380 in the mid-2000s.[23] Airlines like the perceived prestige of operating the latest equipment, but must deal with the teething problems that go along with being the first to embrace the advanced technology. If these problems are severe enough, the reputation of the airplane can suffer thereby hurting future sales. As a result, Airbus and Boeing are looking at incremental improvements to existing aircraft (the A330neo in the first instance, and the B737Max and B777X in the second) as the way to best exploit the huge market potential with a minimum of risk.[24]

Their strategy seems to be working, if current orders are any indication. Airbus narrowly beat Boeing in 2014 in the annual race to book new orders for jetliners, though the European firm delivered fewer aircraft than its rival. Airbus said it booked 1,456 net aircraft orders in 2014, after taking 1,503 net orders in 2013. Similarly, Boeing received 1,432 net orders in 2014. Both have backlogs of orders stretching through the end of the decade for some of their most popular plane models, which can, in truth, be somewhat of a double-edged sword. Airbus, for example, is trying to figure out how to speed up its various production lines to meet the demand. But the challenge is daunting, as the examination of just one product line illustrates. The company currently has 778 firm orders for their A350, which has a production rate of slightly more than one per month. Though that number will increase to 10 over the next three years or so, customers will still have to wait more than seven years for delivery.[25] Amid the order frenzy, doubts are growing about how long the boom in commercial aircraft demand can last, considering the economic slowdown in some growth markets and huge order backlogs. Some industry analysts believe a slump in jet fuel costs, as oil prices have plummeted since 2013, has made older, less efficient planes economically viable again, reducing the need for airlines to buy new jets.[26]

The effort to develop and market aircraft capable of supersonic flight provides an excellent example of just how dicey the whole process can be. Throughout the 1950s, a supersonic transport (SST) looked like the future of air travel. Serious work on commercial designs started during that period as the first generation of supersonic fighters was entering service. By the early 1960s, the designs had progressed to the point where the approval for production was given, but costs were so high that the government-subsidized programs in Great Britain and France eventually merged their efforts in 1962 to produce Concorde. This partnership set off panic in the U.S. industry, where it was thought that the plane would soon replace all other long-range designs, especially after Pan Am took out purchase options on the Concorde. Congress was soon funding an SST design effort, selecting the existing Lockheed and Boeing designs, to produce an even more advanced, larger, faster, and longer ranged design. The Boeing design was eventually selected for continued work, with design goals of ferrying around 300 passengers and having a cruising speed near Mach 3. Even the Soviet Union set out to produce its own design, the Tu-144. Unfortunately, the entire concept was soon in trouble. The SST in the United States was seen as particularly offensive due to its sonic boom and the potential for its engine exhaust to damage the ozone layer. Both problems affected the thinking of lawmakers, and Congress dropped its funding in 1971, along with banning all overland commercial supersonic flights. Nevertheless, in 1976, Concorde entered commercial service. The U.S. political outcry was so great that New York banned the plane, which effectively destroyed the aircraft's economic prospects—it had been built with the London–New York route in mind. Service was allowed into Washington, DC, and was so popular that New Yorkers were soon complaining because they did not have it. It was not long before Concorde was flying into New York's JFK. Unfortunately, the economics of the aircraft no longer made sense. In the beginning, SSTs were envisioned to compete with long-range aircraft seating 80 to 100 passengers such as the Boeing 707, but with newer models such as the Boeing 747 carrying four times that, the speed and fuel advantages of the SST were washed away.[27] Concordes were only sold to British Airways and Air France, at prices heavily subsidized by the British and French governments. The handwriting was clearly on the wall by the end of the 1990s, but the catastrophic loss of an Air France airplane departing Paris in July 2000 followed shortly thereafter by the terrorist attacks of September 11, 2001 sealed the Concorde's fate. Both Air France and British Airways ceased operating the airplane in 2003, with the last regular passenger flights landed at London Heathrow Airport on Friday, October 24.[28]

The big question with any new design is which airlines will be buying these airplanes? The primary customers for new aircraft are the larger scheduled passenger carriers plus some successful charter firms. There is a distinct trickle-down effect with secondary carriers buying the planes replaced by the larger airlines and third-level airlines purchasing what the secondary companies sell and so on. There is no consensus about how old is too old when it comes to a plane. The FAA and industry safety experts generally believe planes can fly for 30 or more years, as long as they are well maintained and the carriers follow all the manufacturer and regulatory directives that require more frequent inspections and fixes as the planes get older.[29] Boeing offers a full suite of customer support to any carrier operating their aircraft whether they are the first owner or a subsequent one.[30] In 2012, Delta opted to acquire 88 narrow-body Boeing 717s and 49 MD-90s and refurbish them rather than buy new aircraft. Even with the planes' higher fuel and maintenance costs (all were well over 10 years old), Delta figures it is saving at least $1 billion on the MD-90 purchases alone, compared with buying new planes, making them roughly 10 percent cheaper to operate per seat than new 737s.[31]

Conclusion

This chapter discussed the different categories of air carriers and how each functions in the global market. The operations of scheduled for-hire airlines, both passenger and cargo, were presented and followed by a similar discussion of the nonscheduled sector. Private or not-for-hire carriers were then examined and the reasons why a company might elect to perform its own transportation instead of using for-hire transportation were provided. After examining each in detail and highlighting some examples where the operational distinction between airlines is fuzzy, the commercial aircraft manufacturing industry and its close relationship to the airlines were also discussed.

CHAPTER 4

External Forces Affecting Air Carrier Operations

Introduction

Airlines must cope with a myriad of outside forces that can adversely impact their successful attainment of profitability. National and global economic conditions, fuel prices, terrorism, and national politics are just some of the uncontrollable factors that airline managers must deal with on multiple levels. Collectively, these can be examined using a Political, Economic, Social, Technological, Environmental, and Legal (PESTEL) framework, which will provide a broad perspective on opportunities and threats that surround the industry. These factors cannot be controlled by management, but they must be understood if the firm is to prosper in an uncertain world. Each will be defined in the following sections, and some current issues will be explained in detail.

Political and Legal Factors

The airline industry is widely influenced by regulations and restrictions related to international trade, tax policy, and competition. It must also deal with issues like war, terrorism, and the outbreak of diseases such as Ebola. Several major factors have had a profound impact on the airline industry.

Terrorism

Commercial aircraft have long been used by terrorist groups, both state sponsored and otherwise, to promote their causes. The attacks on September 11, 2001, effectively curtailed the demand for air travel for more than a year[1] and forced everyone (airlines, passengers, shippers, plane manufacturers, and governments) to redefine air travel, with security as the number one priority. But this coordinated attack on the United States was certainly not the first instance of airliners being used to make a statement. The first documented case of a person or persons attempting to seize control of an aircraft for purposes other than flying to the original destination occurred in Peru in 1931, an act forever after referred to as "hijacking." From 1931 to 1957, there were fewer than 20 air hijackings worldwide. Several of these were in Eastern Europe by people attempting to flee from Soviet rule there. The year 1958 marked the first of several hijackings *from* Cuba to other destinations, but the problem began escalating in 1961 with the first of many hijackings *to* Cuba. From 1958 to 1967, 40 air hijackings took place worldwide, many of them from the United States to Cuba.

In 1968, a number of significant developments took place. First, the number of hijackings jumped dramatically: nearly as many (31) took place in that year alone as had taken place in the preceding 10 years. Second, the number of places where hijackings were taking place increased substantially. The first (and only) successful hijacking of an El Al aircraft was undertaken by PLO terrorists. There were hijackings in China and India. In 1969, the number of hijackings increased again to 82. It was clear that something had to be done. 1973 marked a significant turning point in air hijacking history. The United States and Cuba entered into a reciprocal agreement to prosecute air hijackers. That, along with similar agreements between other countries, for example, Taiwan and China, more stringent security measures, and better scanning equipment resulted in a decrease in air hijacking. By 1980, the number of hijackings had dropped significantly and has never returned to the pre-1968 level. When Castro abrogated the agreement in 1977, hijackings from the United States to Cuba resumed; when the agreement was restored, the hijackings stopped again. From 1968 through 1977, there were roughly 41 hijackings per year; from 1978 through 1988 there were roughly 26 hijackings per year.[2] There were also a number of instances of aircraft being commandeered for ransom, the most well-known being the Northwest Airlines B727 taken over by a man named D.B. Cooper in November 1971. After demanding and receiving $200,000 in exchange for releasing the aircraft and its passengers, he jumped out of the plane somewhere north of the Oregon border with the money strapped to his body. Though he was never found, some of the money was discovered on a Columbia River Beach near Vancouver, Washington in 1980.[3]

Over the years, hijackers have used the aircraft and its passengers as a means to achieve some objective, be it money, asylum, or the furthering of some political agenda. But the 1980s saw organized terrorist groups turn to the destruction of aircraft as a means of drawing attention to their cause. In June of 1985, Air India Flight 182 exploded off the Irish coast on a flight from Toronto to Delhi, an attack attributed to a Sikh extremist group that was subsequently linked to a bomb explosion at Tokyo's Narita airport believed to be intended for another Air India plane.[4]

Then, on December 21, 1988, a suitcase bomb exploded aboard New York-bound Pan Am Flight 103, killing all 259 passengers and crew members, along with 11 people on the ground in Lockerbie, Scotland. Only one suspect, a Libyan intelligence agent, was ever convicted in connection with the attack, and much mystery still surrounds it.[5] In these cases, there was no hijacking; bombs were loaded onto the aircraft as baggage or cargo. On September 11, 2001, American Airlines Flights 11 and 77, along with United Airlines Flights 175 and 93, were hijacked by 19 Al-Qaeda-affiliated extremists and turned into weapons of mass destruction when they were deliberately flown into buildings: 11 and 175 into the twin towers of the World Trade Center in New York City and 77 into the Pentagon in Washington, DC. Flight 93 crashed into a field in Pennsylvania after passengers revolted and caused the hijackers to lose control. More than 3,000 people were killed including 400 police officers and firefighters.[6]

There have even been at least eight confirmed examples of self-hijacking that occurred when a crew member took over an aircraft, often to commit some act of revenge against the company or a loved one that usually included the perpetrator's suicide. Two were especially egregious. During a flight from Jakarta, Indonesia to Singapore on December 19, 1997, Silk Air Flight 185 crashed in Indonesia after entering a rapid descent. It has been suggested by some, including the U.S. National Transportation Safety Board (NTSB) that the captain may have committed suicide by switching off both flight recorders and intentionally putting the Boeing 737 in a dive, possibly when the first officer had left the flight deck. He had apparently been experiencing various work-related difficulties in the six months prior to the incident. Less than two years later, on October 31, 1999, only half an hour after taking off from JFK Airport in New York, Egypt Air Flight 990 entered a rapid descent, crashing into the Atlantic Ocean some 100 kilometers from Nantucket Island, Massachusetts, killing everyone on board. The descent happened moments after the captain left the flight deck, with investigations suggesting that the relief pilot had intentionally sent it into the ocean. There was, however, no conclusive evidence and the claim was heavily disputed by Egyptian authorities.[7] Not included in this total are two recent accidents still under investigation. Malaysian Airlines Flight 370 disappeared March 8, 2014, on a flight from Kuala Lumpur to Beijing. Absolutely no trace of the aircraft or the 239 souls on board was found until late July 2015, when debris began washing up on Reunion Island off the coast of Madagascar in the Western Indian Ocean, thousands of miles from the plane's last-known position.[8] The extensive time between when the aircraft was declared lost and when the wreckage began appearing suggests that it was carefully guided to an extremely remote area of the southern Indian Ocean where it was carefully set down and quickly sank. Given the skill required to reprogram the flight management system, fly the plane for another seven hours, then set it down in the water without break-up, the most likely culprit is the captain, although that accusation may never be proven.[9] More recently, Germanwings Flight 9525 crashed into the French Alps on March 24, 2015, killing 150 people. All signs point to the accident being a deliberate move by the copilot to commit suicide, although the final accident report has yet to be completed.[10]

Even with soaring skyjacking rates during the 1960s, most airlines opposed the idea of individual passenger screening. Passengers were not required to show an ID. Ticket agents gave each one a once-over, looking for behavior that would-be hijackers might display (lack of eye contact, inadequate concern about their luggage, etc.). If someone exhibited these traits, they might be scanned with an electronic magnetometer before boarding (which happened to only 0.5 percent of passengers). Only suspicious travelers who set off the detector could be frisked. It wasn't until 1973 that universal passenger screenings using x-ray machines and metal detectors were mandated, a task outsourced to contractors who were underpaid and often incompetent. Passengers could arrive as late as 30 minutes before boarding; family and friends could accompany travelers to the gate. People put carry-ons and metal items through an x-ray machine and then passed through a metal detector. Checked bags were inspected only for international flights. Today, the Transportation Security Administration (TSA) runs security operations at all U.S. airports. Only ticketed passengers are permitted into the gate area. Once a traveler is issued a boarding pass, he proceeds to a security checkpoint where a TSA officer inspects his boarding pass and ID. Passengers must remove shoes and jackets and send them through an x-ray machine. Certain electronic items must be removed from their cases and screened individually. Sharp tools are banned and liquids limited to three-ounce containers. Some travelers must pass through both a metal detector and a millimeter-wave scanning device.[11] TSA is constantly reviewing its procedures to improve both the passenger experience and security. In recent years, prescreening and trusted traveler programs have been implemented to provide expedited service to prescreened customers who have registered with TSA. Almost half of U.S. airline passengers now pass through expedited security, which enables inspectors to separate travelers who are known to pose a minimal security risk from others, including people identified to receive more scrutiny based on their travel history or other factors. Although TSA does not conduct passenger screening abroad, it requires airports that serve as the last point of departure to the United States to meet stringent security standards and assesses the security programs of all U.S. and foreign air carriers that serve these locations.[12]

Economic Regulation and Deregulation

Government involvement in the business of transportation will be discussed more fully in the next chapter. As previously discussed, the Airline Deregulation Act of 1978 removed almost all regulations governing the business of air transportation, which were, until that time, controlled by the Civil Aeronautics Board (CAB). Recall that, after deregulation, passengers benefited from additional routes through the hub-and-spoke model, competition increased, and airfares fell. As time has passed, more, but not all, countries have adopted this model as well. However, the U.S. Department of Transportation (DOT) continues to keep a close watch on the competitive landscape in the airline industry in order to protect consumer interest and prevent monopoly.

National Tensions

Sometimes commercial flights are unintentionally caught up in tensions between nations. The most recent example (mentioned in Chapter 2) was Malaysian Airlines Flight 17, a B777, shot down on July 14, 2014, while flying at 33,000 feet over rebel-held territory in eastern Ukraine, killing all 295 passengers and crew aboard. Evidence strongly suggests the aircraft was brought down by a surface-to-air missile fired by pro-Russian separatists.[13] In a similar incident, on September 1, 1983, Korean Airlines (KAL) Flight 007, a B747, was on the last leg of a flight from New York City to Seoul, with a stopover in Anchorage, Alaska. As it approached its final destination, the plane began to veer far off its normal course. In just a short time, the plane flew into Russian airspace and crossed over the Kamchatka Peninsula, where some top-secret Soviet military installations were known to be located. The Soviets sent two fighters to intercept the plane. According to tapes of the conversations between the fighter pilots and Soviet ground control, the fighters quickly located the KAL flight and tried to make contact with the passenger jet. Failing to receive a response, one of the fighters fired a heat-seeking missile. KAL 007 was hit and plummeted into the Sea of Japan. All 269 people on board were killed.[14] Finally, on July 3, 1988, a U.S. Navy ship called the Vincennes was exchanging fire with small Iranian ships in the Persian Gulf where it was stationed to protect oil trade routes. As the American and Iranian ships skirmished, Iran Air Flight 655, an A300, took off from nearby Bandar Abbas International Airport, bound for Dubai. The airport was used by both civilian and military aircraft. The Vincennes mistook the lumbering Airbus A300 civilian airliner for a much smaller and faster F-14 fighter jet, perhaps in the heat of battle or perhaps because the flight allegedly did not identify itself. It fired two surface-to-air missiles, killing all 290 passengers and crew members on board.[15]

Economic Factors

Demand for Air Travel

Economic development worldwide is getting a significant boost from air transport. This wider economic benefit is being generated by increasing connections between cities that enable the flow of goods, people, capital, technology, and ideas while reducing air transport costs. The number of unique city-pair connections is estimated at more than 16,000, almost double the connectivity by air 20 years ago. The price of air transport to users continues to fall, after adjusting for inflation. Compared to 20 years ago, real transport costs have more than halved. Governments have also gained substantially from the good performance of the airline industry. Airlines and their customers are forecast to generate $116 billion in tax revenues in 2015. Air transport is vital for manufacturers' trade today, which is more in components rather than finished goods. Finally, the industry continues to create high value-added jobs internally and externally, as spending ripples through manufacturing and travel-related industries.[16]

When a nation's economy is strong, airlines thrive. The reverse happens when the economy is weak. The global recession of 2008–2009 was the deepest since the 1930s and one that hurt all airlines regardless of nationality. International premium passenger numbers fell almost 20 percent between January 2008 and January 2009, while international freight–ton kilometers dropped close to 25 percent over the same period. Global manufacturing plummeted between 15 to 30 percent depending on location, which meant those firms abruptly stopped shipping.[17] The effects of the recession stretched into 2011 and 2012. In order to survive, airlines have had to merge with financially solvent competitors resulting in a much smaller marketplace. In the United States, 10 airlines controlled more than 90 percent of capacity in 2000, but by 2012 those 10 became five through mergers. The five airlines—US Airways (which has since merged with American), Delta, American, Southwest, and United—now control 85 percent of U.S. capacity. The number of scheduled flights dropped 14 percent between 2007 and 2012, as operations were consolidated. In addition, this period saw significant fare increases along with the initiation of what would become a torrent of ancillary fees like baggage charges whereby the carriers began charging for services that had been free.[18]

These and other airline actions have had a significant impact on the industry as a whole, as well as the traveling public. Specifically, airlines have become more aggressive in adjusting fares and flights to respond to fluctuations in fuel prices and demand and have become more profitable as a result. At the same time, the travel experience for the flying public has changed both positively and negatively. For example, there has been a significant reduction in flight delays and cancellations in recent years. Yet there has also been a significant reduction in service at some hub airports and in short-haul flights (i.e., less than 500 miles), which in turn is limiting the choices of many air travelers.[19] Unfortunately, the recession exacerbated the effects of an already dismal decade with the result that the legacy airlines (Alaska, American, Continental, Delta, Northwest, United, and US Airways) lost $62.8 billion by the end of 2009.[20] Ultimately, the changes in the number of airlines controlling the industry, fare increases, and capacity reductions that began in 2008 were not a brief phase, but rather signs of a greater shift in the industry that would redefine carrier operations.

In contrast, the future is much brighter today. According to the International Air Transportation Association (IATA), consumers will see a substantial increase in the value they derive from air transport in 2015. New destinations are up 1.7 percent for the year so far, and frequencies have risen by even more. The organization expects 1 percent of world GDP to be spent on air transport in 2015, totaling more than $760 billion. The demand for air travel is increasing, with growth of 6.7 percent expected this year, the best since 2010, well above the 5.5 percent trend of the past 20 years. This improvement is being driven mainly by the upturn of the economic cycle. But price is also attracting consumers. The average return fare (before surcharges and tax) of $429 in 2015 is forecast to be more than 64 percent lower than 20 years earlier, after adjusting for inflation. Airline executives expect growth in passenger services through mid-2016 to be as strong as in 2010 and early 2011. Cargo is also expected to see its strongest growth since 2010 although both projections hinge on increased economic activity that could be dampened by continued monetary troubles in Europe and Asia.[21] The airlines certainly see to share this view. Airbus and Boeing left the 2015 Paris Air Show with $107 billion in orders for new planes,[22] perhaps in anticipation of longer-term forecasts that predict the demand for air travel will double by the year 2035.[23]

Fuel Prices

Fuel is the largest expense category for airlines,[24] as well as being the least stable. The average price paid by U.S. airlines for a gallon of fuel was $2.06 at the end of First Quarter 2015, down from $3.15 in 2012.[25] Globally, the airlines' fuel bill in 2015 is expected to fall to $191 billion, which will represent 28 percent of their total operating costs, down from 32 percent in 2014. Fuel is such a large and volatile cost that it focuses intense effort in the industry to improve fuel efficiency through replacing aging fleets with new aircraft, improving flight operations, and increasing efforts to persuade governments to remove the airspace and airport inefficiencies that waste around 5 percent of fuel burn each year.[26] However, as all of these actions are potentially expensive and long-term fixes, some carriers have explored other innovative ways of coping with unstable fuel costs.

Purchase Where the Price Is Lowest

Airlines with extensive overseas routes may find it worthwhile to purchase more fuel than they otherwise would at stops in countries where the cost is low. The disadvantage is that the airplane becomes a tanker transporting more fuel than is required for the flight, thereby increasing its weight and operating costs.

Hedging

Hedging[27] is, simply put, like a home insurance policy that is purchased in case something bad happens. The buyer hopes he doesn't need it, but if he does, it's there. Fuel (or more accurately, oil) hedging is similar. Fuel prices shooting up is the "something bad" as it increases airlines' costs significantly. Of course, oil hedging is far more complicated than just buying a home insurance policy, and there are a lot of different ways to do it.

The basic insurance type of policy is when airlines purchase the right to buy oil at a set price at some point in the future. If the price of oil has increased, they can use that option to buy oil at the original, lower price. If oil price has reduced, then the option simply served as an insurance policy that did not get used. The problem here is that with the price of oil being so volatile over the past few years, the cost of simply locking in a fixed price has gone up. Since it's more risky, the financial institutions selling the options need to be paid more to make it worth their while. That's why other types of hedging have become popular. They help lower the cost to the airlines, but they also require that the airlines assume more risk.

One of these techniques is for airlines to enter into an agreement where they are protected from rising prices as shown previously, but they also give up the potential benefit of oil prices going down. Delta, for example, had this type of hedging in the first quarter of 2011 with an average range of $75 to $90 a barrel. This means that if oil stays in that range, Delta gets no benefit. But if oil goes to $100 a barrel, the airline wouldn't end up paying more than $90 a barrel. If, however, oil goes down to $65, then Delta would still have to pay $75.

Another type of bet that airlines make eliminates this range and focuses on one number. For United, this was the largest type of hedge it used in the first quarter of 2011 when it made a bet with financial institutions that oil would stay above an average of $82.65 a barrel. If it did not increase above that number, then the financial institutions would pay United the difference between $82.65 and whatever the airline ended up paying for oil. Had the price fallen under $82.65, then United would have had to pay the difference to the financial institutions. Southwest found itself in a similar situation in 2008. After locking in its oil at a low price, it had a massive cost advantage against the other airlines. The problem is that those low oil prices didn't prevent Southwest from having to adjust to the new realities of higher oil. It simply delayed it until the hedges ran out, and then kept buying hedges at higher and higher prices. When oil prices came crashing back down, Southwest owed a lot of money to the financial institutions with which it made its bets and ran into a cash crunch as a result.

Clearly, oil hedging itself doesn't come without risk, won't necessarily guarantee a set oil price for the airlines, and can be expensive. The most conservative hedging options have a high fixed cost to buy the options. The more risky techniques might not have high fixed costs, but they come with steeper downsides, as Southwest and others learned in 2008 after oil prices fell. That is why you don't see any airlines hedge all of their fuel needs. Even the most aggressive hedging airline still is fully exposed for a third of its fuel needs and doesn't necessarily have a fixed price for the rest. This means that when fuel prices increase, airline costs increase as well. So fare increases are bound to follow.

As crude oil and jet fuel prices continue to decline, many airlines are adapting their fuel hedging strategies to account for the lower price environment that began in 2013. On one hand, companies like Thai Airways are adopting a more aggressive stance or beginning to hedge their fuel price exposure for the first time in company history. Others are emulating Etihad Airways by taking a step back and either reducing the scale of their hedging programs or eliminating them completely. Finally, some others like United are taking an entirely different approach, choosing to sell their existing positions (and realize the losses) in order to enter into new positions at lower prices. There isn't a "one size fits all" approach to hedging that works for all companies. As the aforementioned examples indicate, the best fuel hedging strategy for an airline, or any company for that matter, is the one that best suits its risk tolerance, hedging objectives, financial position, and so on. While many hedging strategies might appear to provide an ideal solution, the details are often much more complex.[28]

Supply Chain Integration

In 2012, Delta Airlines initiated a rather unique hedging strategy by purchasing its own oil refinery, an aging and mothballed ConocoPhillips plant located in Trainer, Pennsylvania (just outside Philadelphia), for $180 million. At the time, the carrier had a vast jet fuel logistics chain with storage terminals, pipeline capacity, and a team of energy traders. Oil prices were more than $90 a barrel and its planes were burning the equivalent of 260,000 barrels a day, representing a third of total costs. By making jet fuel in the company's own facility, management hoped to recoup some of the $2.2 billion it figured was going to refiners as profit. To date, Delta has invested $420 million of capital into the refinery, which has generated roughly $100 million of losses. While the airline expects to pay about $0.50 a gallon less in 2015, it's only because oil prices have plunged and has nothing to do with owning a refinery. Besides, the real test is to compare Delta's fuel costs to those of other big airlines. Before the acquisition, Delta was sourcing fuel for $0.09 a gallon cheaper than its peers. Its edge today: still $0.09. Meanwhile, much of its rationale for owning a refinery has disappeared: refiners' margins have declined, while American crude no longer sells at such a wide discount to imported barrels. In the crystal ball of hindsight, Delta would have been better off just waiting for oil prices to fall and then locking in lower fuel prices in the futures market. Instead it's stuck with an expensive albatross.[29] The big risk with supply chain integration, especially via ownership of a partner, is that it takes the company into an industry beyond its core competency. Few would dispute Delta's excellence as an airline, but that expertise does not extend to oil refining, as the results of its strategy show.

Stay the Course

Hedging, like any other form of insurance, requires the carrier to incur costs that essentially raise the price per gallon paid for fuel. After crude oil prices hit an all-time high of $147 in mid-July 2008, US Airways' top leaders decided to drop their historic practice of hedging. In other words, they would pay the market price for jet fuel without the use of any strategies discussed earlier. They brought that same philosophy to American Airlines Group Inc., created in early 2014 by the merger of US Airways and American Airlines. American historically had invested in fuel-based hedges, but the new leadership, drawn mainly from US Airways, had sold off the last of American's hedges by the middle of that year. In the years leading up to 2008, American Airlines usually paid less than US Airways for a gallon of jet fuel. But with the exception of

2011, US Airways paid less per gallon each year since, than American and most other carriers as well. The biggest advantage came in 2009 as fuel prices were plummeting and airlines holding hedges lost money on the investments. US Airways paid an average of $1.74 a gallon that year, compared with $2.01 for American, $2.15 for Delta Air Lines, $1.80 for United Airlines Inc., and $2.12 for Southwest Airlines Co. In 2013, US Airways' advantage over American was only a nickel: $3.04 per gallon vs. $3.09. But with the oceans of jet fuel that airlines burn each year, small differences can mean big dollars. In 2013, each penny in the price of a gallon of jet fuel represented $28.1 million in expenses at American and $11.4 million at US Airways. If American could have saved that nickel, it would have reduced its costs by $140 million. US Airways would have paid $57 million more for fuel if it had paid American's average cost per gallon.[30]

Social and Demographic Factors

Categorizing generations in the United States according to the year of birth provides insight into the changing trends in the travel and tourism industry. The demand for air travel has increased significantly over the years. This indicates changing travel preferences among the latest generation. The U.S. population is categorized as follows:

- Baby boom generation—Born between 1946 and 1964
- Generation X—Born between 1965 and 1979
- Generation Y or Millennial generation—Born between 1980 and 1999
- Generation Z—Born after 2000

These segments also play an important role in forecasting demand because they match customer expectations in regard to value-add service offerings. For example, in the United States, the future of travel and tourism will be defined by the growth in the millennial generation. In the next five to ten years, they will enter their peak earning, spending, and traveling years. Their spending on business travel is expected to grow by 50 percent of the total by 2020 and to remain strong for the next 15 years after that. Currently, the baby boomers are the active customers. Their business travel spending is expected to decline to 16 percent by 2020 and to 11 percent by 2025.

Globally, the fast emergence of a new middle class in developing countries will add to aviation demand. Together these two trends will change the dynamics of how people and trade move by air around the world with new flows, new routes, and a shift in emphasis between existing routes. Over the next 20 years, the airline industry is expecting to triple or quadruple its services in order to serve the demand for air travel and cargo services. This growth appears to be generated by the expansion of the middle-income classes in Asia Pacific and emerging economies in Latin America, Middle East, and North Africa (MENA), and Sub-Saharan Africa.[31]

Technological Factors

Technological advancement has been the driving factor for improving airlines' operational efficiency. Airlines have been able to reduce costs and improve operations by using advanced aircraft design and engine technology, IT solutions, and mobile technology that has created better connectivity and enhanced passengers' travel experience. The increased use of composite materials in the construction process worked in concert with enhanced engine performance to increase payload and range while reducing emissions and noise. In fact, two-engine airliners are rapidly replacing four-engine models because they can cover virtually all long-distance routes at much lower cost.

Environmental Factors

The global aviation industry consumes more than 200 million tons of fuel per year. The rising demand for air transport and the rising crude oil prices could impact the industry's carbon emissions. The environmental impact could also influence sustainability. According to the Air Transport Action Group (ATAG), the airline industry's impact on the environment is as follows:

- The global aviation industry processes 2 percent of all human-induced carbon dioxide (CO_2) emissions. Air travel is responsible for 12 percent of the total emissions from the transportation industry.
- Alternative fuels, like sustainable biofuels, are expected to reduce the aviation carbon footprint of fuel by 80 percent.
- Eighty percent of the CO_2 emissions are from flights that are longer than 1,500 kilometers.

Sustainable alternative jet fuels can help to address challenges arising from fuel cost, pollution, and energy security. Their use could reduce emissions that impact surface air quality and global climate while expanding domestic energy sources that diversify fuel supplies, contribute to price and supply stability, and generate economic development in rural communities. The Federal Aviation Administration (FAA) is working to enable the United States use of one billion gallons per year of "drop-in" sustainable alternative jet fuels by 2018. Though they are created from renewable sources, drop-in fuels mimic the chemistry of petroleum jet fuel, can be used in today's aircraft and engines without modification, and provide the same level of performance and safety as today's petroleum-derived jet fuel.[32]

Conclusion

The plethora of uncontrollable factors that can impact an airline, positively or negatively, is almost overwhelming. For carriers serving global markets, coping with uncontrollable and often rapidly unfolding events is a "normal" management task. Contingency plans are absolutely essential, both for identifying areas of opportunity and for dealing with events that can negatively impact operations. This chapter looked at some of these factors, and discussed future implications for airlines and aircraft manufacturers.

CHAPTER 5

Government Involvement in Airline Operations

Introduction

In this chapter, you will learn how governments oversee the many facets of air transportation. As mentioned in Chapter 1, governments typically must exercise some degree of influence over the business of transportation to ensure the needs of the public are met by (a) guarding against the monopolistic tendencies of the railroads and pipelines, and (b) preventing destructive competition in the airline, trucking, and water carrier industries. The role of government in the airline business will be presented as will the ongoing government involvement in other aspects of the airline industry, namely security, safety, environmental issues, and infrastructure support.

Business

Economic Regulation in the United States

As the first modern mode of transportation, railroads deserve special attention because nations often dealt with the subsequent development of the other modes the same way as they did with rail. Interestingly, in the earliest years, railroads were often private firms regardless of which country they were in. In the United States, while the early development mirrored what was going on elsewhere, the later years did not. The U.S. companies have always been privately owned (with one exception that will be discussed later), and remain so today. In fact, the United States has virtually the only completely private railroad industry (infrastructure and operations) in the world. However, this situation has been somewhat problematic over the years as the monopolistic power of the railroads was often abused. Between 1850 and the mid-1880s, the railroads became increasingly powerful as they expanded westward across the country. They could charge whatever prices they wished, serve whom they chose, and generally discriminate in whatever way suited their purposes.

By 1887, the U.S. government had had enough and began regulating the business aspects of the railroads. A special federal agency, the Interstate Commerce Commission (ICC), was established just for that purpose. If a railroad wanted to start a new service, abandon unprofitable routes, change its pricing, merge with another company, or make any number of other changes that would be considered normal management decisions in any other industry, it had to seek the permission of the ICC. If the ICC denied their request, the company's only recourse was to sue them. Even then, there was no guarantee the courts would overturn the decision. Similarly, shippers could lodge complaints with the ICC against the railroads in cases where unfair practices were alleged. Again, the parties could either abide by the ICC's ruling or sue. In any case, these proceedings were expensive and extremely time consuming, often taking a decade or more to be resolved.

The government also sought to extend rail services to as much of the United States as possible, both to knit the states more closely together and to foster national commerce. Obviously, if left alone, the railroads would only serve profitable routes. To ensure that all markets would have rail access, the ICC strictly controlled the awarding of routes. The number of carriers allowed to serve a profitable route was limited, and those that were permitted had to agree to serve a money-losing route as well. The end result was that competition was turned upside-down: profitable routes had less competition and higher prices while unprofitable ones had more competition and lower prices, just the opposite of what a free market would dictate. In other words, the government was happy: the railroads were effectively prevented from earning excessive profits (the income from the lucrative routes offset the losses from the money losers, providing the railroads with a "fair return" on their investment), and rail services were provided to a huge area of the country.

All of the other modes in the United States were regulated in exactly the same way: pipelines in 1906, trucking in 1935, airlines in 1938, and domestic water carriers in 1940. All but commercial air transport were placed under the authority of the ICC who used the same model with them as with the railroads: firms had to receive permission to operate, add or drop services, change prices, and so on. In fact, the air carriers were almost included under the ICC as well, but ended up with their own agency, the Civil Aeronautics Board (CAB), that implemented similar requirements. Note that all of the modes were regulated when they were relatively new, but for dramatically different reasons. Railroads and pipelines were controlled to protect shippers from their monopolistic power; truck, water, and air carriers were regulated to protect the carriers themselves from excessive competition. The government's view was that, if left alone, transportation industries tended to gravitate to one of two extremes: monopolistic power or destructive competition. Both were deemed to be unhealthy for the nation, so the government stepped in to protect the public with economic regulation and thereby ensure the development of a strong national transportation system. Most other nations in the world dealt with these same issues by simply owning, operating, or controlling the various forms of transportation.

Economic Deregulation in the United States

By the mid-1970s, serious questions were being asked in government about the continued efficacy of economic regulation. There were concerns that the world had changed and that shippers and passengers were paying higher prices than they should under what had become an antiquated system. The United States was the first nation to free the modes from governmental interference in their operations: air cargo in 1977, passenger airlines in 1978, and railroads and trucking companies in 1980. This national paradigm shift, now referred to in general as deregulation, placed the business of transportation back into the hands of managers who, for better or worse, were now responsible for the success or failure of their own enterprises. Companies were now free to start new services, abandon unprofitable routes, set their own prices (within certain limitations), and generally take control of their own destinies. As a result, pricing became rationalized, falling on competitive routes and rising on those with lower demand.

Initially, new carriers proliferated in the airline industries, fares fell as the added competition took effect, and many communities lost scheduled air services as firms abandoned unprofitable routes. As time passed, company failures became common as firms—some new and others that had been in business for decades—were simply unable to adjust to the rigors of competition. Customers, be they shippers or passengers, after enjoying lower freight rates and airfares for a while, realized that, in fact, you do get what you pay for. Goods were often lost or damaged, delivery dates were missed, onboard flight amenities that most people had taken for granted began to disappear, and the companies focused on cutting costs to improve their profitability. Thus, customers gradually learned that the lowest price alternative was not always the best and that paying for higher levels of service was necessary to ensure customer satisfaction. Generally speaking, deregulation has been a success. Airline passengers often complain about the austere nature of air travel today, but more people are flying than ever before. All of the modes are better able to tailor their service offerings to the needs of their customers and set their prices accordingly. But as in any free market, you buy what you can afford, which may be quite different from what you want, a situation that breeds dissatisfaction. The airlines are especially bedeviled by this problem: passengers want first-class service at coach prices, and complain when they do not get it. Reconciling customer expectations with reality is a constant battle for managers in a deregulated environment and will be discussed further in the next chapter.

Regulation and Deregulation in Europe

European airlines evolved in much the same way as those in the United States, except that they were government owned from the beginning of the industry in the 1920s. Each nation regardless of size had its own carrier with routes that spanned the globe. For countries with larger internal travel markets, there were often two state-run airlines: one (or more) providing domestic and intra-European services, the other providing long-distance international coverage (e.g., British European Airways [BEA] and British Overseas Airways Corporation [BOAC] in Great Britain). As time passed, small privately owned operators emerged as well to exploit markets of no interest to the government-run competition, but were relatively insignificant until the mid-1980s.

In December 1987, the European Council of Ministers took the first important step toward the creation of a common air transport policy for the European Economic Community (EEC) with the adoption of the First Package of legislative measures dealing with aviation matters between Member States. Issues dealt with included, among other things, rules on fares for scheduled air services, the sharing of passenger capacity between air carriers on scheduled services, and access for air carriers to scheduled air service routes. The Second Package in July 1990 built on the first by introducing an element of "double disapproval" for fares, under which a fare set by an airline for a route between Member States would be permitted unless both States disapproved it. This applied to applications for increases in fares above five percent. The Second Package also opened up routes between almost all Community airports, relaxed restrictions on beyond services, and eased restrictions on designation of multiple airlines on particular routes. It is only with the Third Aviation Liberalization Package in 1992 that a substantially liberalized internal Community market was achieved.[1] Beginning in 1993, any airline licensed by any of the European Union (EU) member states was considered to be a "Community Air Carrier" and was free to carry passengers, mail, and cargo throughout the EU, although the license does not entitle the owner to serve a particular route. In addition, a carrier may charge whatever fare it wants without government oversight simply by filing notice of the change. Finally, the Commission adopted State Aid guidelines that strictly controlled the amount of financial support a government could provide to its airline, a move intended to decrease national protection of domestic firms and increase competition.[2] Since that time, many new carriers have entered the market while some established national airlines have failed (Sabena in Belgium and Swissair in Switzerland), merged (Air France–KLM), or been taken over by foreign companies (Alitalia by Etihad).

Summary Comments

When viewed globally, the extent of airline economic regulation and deregulation is a continuum with the United States (and others) embracing open competition at one end, states like North Korea with no competition whatsoever at the other, and a host of different models in between. Even in open markets, governments must ensure airlines, like every business, operate fairly and within the law. For example, in the United States, the Department of Transportation (DOT) has responsibility for handling vestigial regulatory questions, while existing agencies and laws dealing with, for example, antitrust or pricing issues as they pertain to all businesses are deemed sufficient for airline matters as well. In fact, the Department of Justice is currently investigating whether U.S. airlines colluded on expansion plans, amid concerns from consumer advocates and politicians that the industry is trying to extend its recent run of prosperity by controlling capacity to keep airfares high.[3]

Security

United States

The entire world of commercial aviation was upended with the terrorist attacks in New York City on September 11, 2001. Eleven days after that awful day, Pennsylvania Governor Tom Ridge was appointed as the first Director of the Office of Homeland Security. The office oversaw and coordinated a comprehensive national strategy to safeguard the country against terrorism and respond to any future attacks. With the passage of the Homeland Security Act by Congress in November 2002, the Department of Homeland Security (DHS) formally came into being as a stand-alone, Cabinet-level department to further coordinate and unify national homeland security efforts, opening its doors on March 1, 2003.[4] All or part of 22 different federal departments and agencies were brought into the new organization, including U.S. Customs and Border Protection (CBP), U.S. Immigration and Customs Enforcement, Transportation Security Administration (TSA), Federal Emergency Management Agency (FEMA), the U.S. Coast Guard, and U.S. Secret Service, just to name a few.[5]

Until recently, the TSA had applied relatively uniform methods to screen airline passengers, focusing primarily on advances in screening technology to improve security and efficiency. TSA has recently shifted away from this approach, which assumes a uniform level of risk among all airline travelers, to one that focuses more intently on those thought to pose elevated security risks. Risk-based passenger screening includes a number of initiatives that fit within a broader framework addressing security risks, but specifically emphasizes the detection and management of potential threats posed by certain people. As mentioned in an earlier chapter, various risk-based approaches to airline passenger screening have been used since the early 1970s, including the application of rudimentary behavioral profiles, security questions, and analysis of ticket purchase data to look for indicators of heightened risk. Additionally, "no-fly" lists were developed to prevent known or suspected terrorists from boarding aircraft, but prior to the terrorist attacks on September 11, 2001, these lists were not robust and proved ineffective.[6]

Following the 9/11 attacks, TSA's initial risk-based efforts focused on integrating checks of passenger name records against the "no fly" list of individuals to be denied boarding and the "selectee" list of individuals of elevated risk requiring more thorough secondary screening. These efforts culminated in the deployment of Secure Flight, which screens each passenger's full name and date of birth against terrorist watch lists. Additionally, international passengers are screened by U.S. CBP, which uses the Advance Passenger Information System (APIS) and the Automated Targeting System-Passenger (ATS-P) to conduct risk assessments. At airports, TSA employs behavioral detection and analysis under the Screening Passengers by Observational Techniques (SPOT) program in an effort to identify suspicious passengers. Another risk-based security program is Pre-Check, a trusted traveler program designed to expedite processing of low-risk passengers. In addition to the Pre-Check participants, TSA is routing certain other passengers through expedited lanes using behavior detection officers and canine teams to screen for suspicious behavior and explosives under an initiative called managed inclusion.[7]

Despite their sophistication, all of these systems rely not only on physical screening with various machines, but on profiling passengers who fit a certain description based upon their flight origins or destinations or frequencies, behavior, ethnic origin, or physical appearance. As long as a person does not set off one of these checks, they are passed through. Conversely, people who fit a certain profile are constantly stopped and subjected to increased scrutiny, even when none of these inspections reveal anything suspect. Thus, the TSA is in the unenviable position of having to quickly conduct thorough screenings while offending as few people as possible. TSA security efforts extend to the air as well. Their Federal Air Marshal Service places trained law enforcement professionals on many flights that blend in with passengers and rely on their training, including investigative techniques, criminal terrorist behavior recognition, firearms proficiency, aircraft specific tactics, and close quarters self-defense measures to protect the flying public.[8] While the exact number of daily flights covered by U.S. air marshals is not publicly known, 5 percent seems to be a widely held number, although some say it could be fewer than that.[9]

In an effort to identify potential threats as early in the travel process as possible, TSA has identified 10 "countries of interest" (Afghanistan, Algeria, Iraq, Lebanon, Libya, Nigeria, Pakistan, Saudi Arabia, Somalia, and Yemen)[10] and three nations on the State Department's list of countries that sponsor terrorism (Iran, Sudan, and Syria).[11] Most of the countries being targeted do not have direct flights to the United States, but passengers whose trips begin in those countries will face extra screening at airports where they board U.S.-bound flights.[12]

Around the World

While certain security measures such as bag searches and the obligatory walk through a metal detector are practically universal, security procedures are by no means uniform across the world. Certain countries have unique security routines at the airport that might seem strange, annoying, or downright offensive to foreign visitors.[13] Israel, for example, is more concerned with conducting a thorough inspection than with minimizing passenger discomfort. Contrary to most of the rest of the world, Israel relies more on personal scrutiny of, and interaction with, each and every passenger than they do technology. El Al, the Israeli national airline, is widely considered the world's most secure, a designation that comes with certain costs. First, the carrier ignores political correctness. Critics of El Al's practices like to denounce their passenger security checks because they include racial profiling. They have a policy of singling out young Arab men for extensive search procedures—but that's playing the odds. When there is a tight schedule, time doesn't need to be wasted searching low-risk people. Second, passengers are thoroughly interviewed before boarding all

El Al flights. Psychologists believe very few potential terrorists are able to stay calm during direct questioning right before boarding the flight. People trained in interrogation are able to tell if passengers are nervous or lying. While airline employees may ask if someone packed their bags themselves, they aren't trained to read a person's eye movements and facial twitches. El Al staff is trained and ask the reason for a passenger's trip, his job or occupation, and whether he has packed his bags himself. In fact, the airline directs its economy class passengers to arrive at the airport three hours before departure to allow sufficient time for the check-in process.[14] Other unique aspects of flying on El Al include double-reinforced cockpit doors, the use of an infrared countermeasures system that protects the plane from heat-seeking missiles, and the presence of air marshals on every flight.[15]

Brazilian airports have security issues that don't involve flying. Professional thieves haunt the airports and look for bags to snatch when passengers aren't paying attention. The thieves also work in teams. One person will distract a passenger while the other person steals the passenger's bag. Watching baggage very closely is a security measure that people traveling through Brazilian airports must take. For Saudi Arabia, airport security begins before travelers reach the airport. Saudi Arabia has strict controls on who may enter the country, and foreigners must get a visa in advance. Citizens of Israel and anyone possessing a passport with an Israeli stamp aren't allowed to visit Saudi Arabia. Women traveling to or from Saudi Arabian airports are also subject to strict rules. If they aren't met at the airport by a husband, male relative, or sponsor, they will not be permitted to leave the airport. In order to exit Saudi Arabia, a married woman must get prior permission from her husband. An unmarried woman can't catch a flight out of Saudi Arabia without the written consent of her father or male guardian. Plus, there are very strict rules about what can be transported into the country. At the airport, customs officials will search passengers' bags for forbidden items such as alcohol, pork products, and pornography.[16]

Summary Comments

From the aforementioned discussion, it is obvious that the idea of airport security is often shaped by cultural beliefs and values and societal preoccupations of the countries in which it is enacted. Furthermore, security on domestic flights in some areas of the world may be perfunctory at best. In addition, the lack of uniformity in processes even between developed nations is somewhat surprising. Passengers departing from Frankfurt, for example, travelling to America will go through a security check in Germany that does not require the removal of footwear. Upon arriving at the U.S. gateway airport (i.e., Atlanta), they process through immigration and customs inspections. Once completed, and despite the fact that they have been in a secure environment since the security check in Europe, passengers must be rescreened by TSA, to include taking off their shoes, before being allowed entry into the terminal for onward movement. While no one would argue with the need for these checks, even seasoned travelers can find them frustrating and time consuming at times.

Safety

Introduction

The International Civil Aviation Organization (ICAO) is a UN specialized agency, created in 1944 upon the signing of the Convention on International Civil Aviation (Chicago Convention).

ICAO works with the Convention's 191 Member States and global aviation organizations to develop international Standards and Recommended Practices (SARPs), which States reference when developing their legally enforceable national civil aviation regulations.[17] ICAO was originally created to promote the safe and efficient development of civil aviation. One enduring aspect of the Organization's work over the last six decades has been to help States improve their civil aviation in their country through projects implemented under ICAO's Technical Cooperation Program. Since its creation in 1952, the Technical Cooperation Bureau (TCB) has been responsible for the execution of the Technical Cooperation Program advising and assisting States, donors, the private sector, and other funding sources in all matters relating to the development of safe and secure civil aviation.[18] Recall that international air rights are *voluntarily* exchanged between nations; that is, each country gives the other permission to provide services. As a part of that arrangement, each government is permitted to request consultation with the other regarding the safety of crews, aircraft, and airline operations, and to revoke, suspend, limit, or impose conditions on the operating authorizations or technical permissions of a carrier that has failed to comply with applicable laws and regulations.[19] Thus, under the broad umbrella of the ICAO, each nation is ultimately responsible for the safe operation of its own airline industry.

Aviation Safety Oversight in the United States

The Federal Aviation Administration (FAA), a part of the U.S. DOT, is responsible for overseeing all aspects of the American aviation industry. The Aviation Safety Office is responsible for the certification, production approval, and continued airworthiness of aircraft, as well as certification of pilots, mechanics, and others in safety-related positions. Also in its purview is the certification of all operational and maintenance enterprises in domestic civil aviation, certification and safety oversight of approximately 7,300 U.S. commercial airlines and air operators, civil flight operations, and the development of applicable regulations.[20]

Beginning in mid-1991, the FAA began to formulate a method to address foreign air transportation safety concerns as well. As a result, the International Aviation Safety Assessment (IASA) program was formally established in 1992, with the purpose of ensuring that all foreign air carriers operating to or from the United States, or code sharing with a U.S. carrier, are properly licensed and subject to safety oversight provided by a competent national Civil Aviation Authority (CAA) in accordance with ICAO standards. IASA assessments determine compliance with these international standards by focusing on each critical element (CE) of an effective aviation safety oversight authority specified by the ICAO. These eight CEs include:

- (CE-1) Primary aviation legislation
- (CE-2) Specific operating regulations
- (CE-3) State civil aviation system and safety oversight functions
- (CE-4) Technical personnel qualification and training

- (CE-5) Technical guidance, tools, and the provision of safety critical information
- (CE-6) Licensing, certification, authorization, and approval obligations
- (CE-7) Surveillance obligations
- (CE-8) Resolution of safety concerns[21]

The IASA does not evaluate the safety compliance of any particular air carrier, nor does it address aviation security, airports, or air traffic management. After an in-country assessment by the FAA, the assessment report is written and the nation is placed into one of two categories: Category 1 includes countries that have demonstrated they meet the ICAO standards for each of the eight CEs; Category 2 means that the safety oversight provided by a country's CAA was found noncompliant in at least one of the CEs. Foreign air carriers from countries with an IASA category have the following technical permissions regarding economic authority:

- Carriers from Category 1 countries are permitted to operate into the United States and code share with U.S. air carriers in accordance with DOT authorizations.
- Carriers from Category 2 countries that operate into the United States and code share with U.S. air carriers have such services limited to those that existed at the time of the assessment.
- Carriers from Category 2 countries that seek to initiate commercial service into the United States and seek to code share with any U.S. air carrier are prohibited from initiating such services.

Through the application of the IASA program, the FAA continues to facilitate compliance with international standards, ensure that countries provide proper oversight of each air carrier operating into the United States or code sharing with a U.S. air carrier, meet the statutory requirements of Congress for aviation safety, and meet expectations of the traveling public. As a result, the IASA program remains an integral part of the

FAA's continuing mission to provide the safest, most efficient aerospace system in the world.[22]

Aviation Safety Oversight in Europe

In the EU, the aviation safety system is based on a close collaboration between the European Commission, the European Aviation Safety Agency (EASA), Eurocontrol (the EU-wide air traffic control system), national civil aviation authorities, and safety investigation authorities of the Member States, as well as the aircraft manufacturers, airlines, and other participants in the single aviation market. The backbone of this system is a set of common safety rules that are directly applicable in a uniform manner across the EU. They apply both to the industry as well as to the civil aviation authorities and constitute the basis of the initial approval and continuing oversight of all aviation activities within the EU. In addition, any aircraft, European or not, may be subject to safety inspections at the European airports. Such ramp checks are done on a random basis but with particular attention to companies that have previously shown safety deficiencies. A series of safety violations identified during such inspections can subsequently lead to restricting or, in the worst cases, banning the operation of the noncompliant air carriers from flying to Europe. Similarly, the European Commission regularly monitors the safety performance of air carriers around the world and informs European citizens about any potential safety risks.[23]

Summary Comments

Virtually every nation has some type of civil aviation agency. Unfortunately, the lack of consistency in airline safety regulation across borders has very real implications for those who fly to, from, or within certain countries. For example, passengers who fly in third-world areas face 13 times the risk of being killed in an air accident as passengers in the first world. The more economically advanced second-world countries have better overall safety records than the others, but even their death risk per flight is seven times as high as that in first-world countries. Between 2000 and 2007, the chance of dying on a scheduled flight in a first-world nation like the

United States, Japan, or Ireland was 1 in 14 million (this statistic considers propeller planes as well as jets). At that rate, a passenger who took one flight every day would on average go 38,000 years before succumbing to a fatal accident. On the airlines of economically advancing countries in the developing world such as Taiwan, India, and Brazil, the death risk per flight was 1 in 2 million. In less economically advanced developing world countries, the death risk per flight was 1 in 800,000.[24] As was discussed in an earlier chapter, there are parts of the world where air travel is virtually unregulated and extremely risky. The preceding statistics certainly bear that out.

Environmental Issues

Internationally, the ICAO has long been the forum for evaluating the environmental performance of aircraft engines. It has taken a "technology progressing" approach, raising standards within the capabilities of proven technologies and certified products (engines and aircraft) rather than a "technology forcing" approach, which would set standards based on technology that is not certified or may not even exist. The reason for ICAO's approach is quite simple—the very high premium placed on the safety of aircraft operation restricts the use of unproven new technologies. The three main environmental issues in the aviation industry are air pollution, noise pollution, and climate change. The first two have improved dramatically over the years as advances in engine technology have resulted in less polluting and quieter aircraft operations. Unfortunately, the attendant increase in the demand for air transportation has dramatically increased the number of planes operating around the world. In addition, the impact of aviation on climate change is still not completely understood, so governments are approaching the issue of pollution from different angles.

The United States has emphasized the reduction of air and noise pollution, while the Europeans are more concerned with understanding and dealing with climate change. Other governments may have little concern for any of these issues as they focus more on economic development or other national issues that are simply more important to them than the environment. Because aircraft can remain in service for 30 years or longer, many older models end up in developing or less developed nations that are willing to put up with their higher levels of pollution and noise. The Clean Air Act (CAA) is the primary, overarching air quality law in the United States. The CAA establishes the Environmental Protection Agency (EPA) as the agency responsible for setting appropriate air quality standards and developing regulations to meet these standards.[25]

Thus, the EPA has primary responsibility for aviation emissions, but many federal agencies such as the FAA, Department of Defense (DOD), National Aeronautics and Space Administration (NASA), state, and local agencies, as well as aircraft and engine manufacturers have an interest in the topic as well.

Unfortunately, there is less coordination of these disparate efforts in the United States than in Europe. The European Union Emissions Trading System (EU ETS), also known as the *European Union Emissions Trading Scheme*, was the first large greenhouse gas emissions trading scheme in the world, and remains the biggest. It was launched in 2005 to fight global warming and is a major pillar of EU climate policy. As of 2013, the EU ETS covers more than 11,000 factories, power stations, and other installations with a net heat excess of 20 megawatts in 31 countries—all 28 EU member states plus Iceland, Norway, and Liechtenstein. Under the "cap and trade" principle, a maximum (cap) is set on the total amount of greenhouse gases that can be emitted by all participating organizations. "Allowances" for emissions are then auctioned off or allocated for free, and can subsequently be traded. Companies must monitor and report their CO_2 emissions, ensuring they hand in enough allowances to the authorities to cover their emissions. If emissions exceed what is permitted by its allowances, an organization must purchase allowances from others. Conversely, if an operation has performed well at reducing its emissions, it can sell its leftover credits. This allows the system to find the most cost-effective ways of reducing emissions without significant government intervention.

Aviation emissions were to be included from 2012. The airline industry and other countries whose airlines serve the EU reacted adversely to the inclusion of the aviation sector, primarily because all mileage to and from the EU was to be included in the emissions calculation. These nations argued that the EU did not have jurisdiction to regulate flights when they were not in European skies; China and the United States threatened to ban their national carriers from complying with the scheme. On November 27, 2012, the United States enacted the European Union Emissions Trading Scheme Prohibition Act of 2011, which prohibited U.S. carriers from participating in the ETS. However, the EU insisted that the regulation should be applied equally to all carriers, and that it did not contravene international regulations. In the absence of a global agreement on airline emissions, the EU argued that it was forced to go ahead with its own scheme, which included an exemption clause for countries with "equivalent measures."[26]

In response, the European Parliament agreed to "stop the clock" on the application of ETS to extraterritorial flights allowing the ICAO to begin work on its own global emission plan.[27] The EU Parliament's further extension until 2016 is consistent with the historic agreement reached at the ICAO Assembly in 2013, which rejected unilateral approaches while cementing the global commitment by airlines and governments to continue to work together to address climate change and achieve carbon neutral growth from 2020. The ICAO agreement confirmed that industry and government investments in technology, operations, and infrastructure measures should remain the primary means of further reducing aviation carbon emissions, while establishing a commitment to work toward a global market-based measure to "fill the gap" if needed.[28]

Infrastructure

Airports

Traditionally, many airports around the world were owned and operated by local or national governments. Today, despite decades of privatization of state enterprises, almost 50 percent of the airports in the world are still operated by some level of government. One example of this approach is found in the United States, where, with one exception (Branson, Missouri), commercial airports are owned and operated by public entities, including local, regional, or state authorities with the power to issue bonds to finance some of their capital needs.[29] On the other hand, since the privatization of the three airports in London and four other major airports in the UK and the forming of British Airport Authority (BAA plc) in 1987, many countries have introduced private sector involvement with different degrees of private ownership and management, from 100 percent private operations of the whole airport to subcontracting of management of part of the airport.[30] In fact, nearly half of European air passengers currently travel through airports that are either fully or partially privatized.[31] Nevertheless, there is no one single model that fits all situations in all countries. The choice of model depends very much on the specific circumstances of the airport.

Air Traffic Control

Like airport ownership, air traffic control is handled differently by each nation. As previously mentioned, in the United States, this function is the responsibility of the FAA. During the past two decades, however, nearly 50 governments have gone a different way and privatized their air traffic control systems, a topic that will be discussed more fully in the next chapter. Briefly, these governments have separated their ATC activities from their transport ministries, removed them from the civil service, and made them self-supporting from fees charged to aircraft operators. These new air navigation service providers (ANSPs) are usually regulated at arm's length by their government's aviation safety agency.[32]

Conclusion

Simply put, governments around the world are very much involved in the provision of air transport services. Some elect to control the business aspects of their airlines, while others like the United States are relying on the free market to allocate air transport services. In both cases, however, issues pertaining to airline security, safety, environmental impacts, and infrastructure also have ramifications for society as a whole, necessitating ongoing government involvement in the industry.

CHAPTER 6

Opportunities and Challenges for the Industry

Introduction

Moving forward, the airline industry will face many opportunities and challenges. Opportunities include expanding markets as demand for air travel increases in nations such as China and India, as well as those in Africa. Indeed, as the global economy continues to improve, the demand for air travel in general should increase as people once again have the discretionary income to travel. As global trade continues to grow and supply chains tighten, air freight will become more attractive as a way to meet customer needs without maintaining inventory. Threats to the successful exploitation of these opportunities include infrastructure limitations, fuel cost volatility, increasing global competition, and growing levels of customer dissatisfaction.

Opportunities

Future Demand for Air Transportation

Passenger Travel

The International Air Transport Association (IATA) is projecting that passenger numbers are expected to reach 7.3 billion by 2034. That represents a 4.1 percent average annual growth in demand for air connectivity that will result in more than a doubling of the 3.3 billion passengers expected to travel in 2014. China will overtake the United States as the world's largest passenger market (defined by traffic to, from, and within) by 2030. Both markets, however, are expected to remain the largest by a wide margin. In 2034, flights to, from, and within China will account for some 1.3 billion passengers, 856 million more than 2014 with an average annual growth rate of 5.5 percent. Traffic to, from, and within the United States is expected to grow at an average annual growth rate of 3.2 percent, which will see 1.2 billion passengers by 2034 (559 million more than 2014). The Association's Global Passenger Forecast Report explains future trends in passenger numbers by means of three key demand drivers: living standards, population and demographics, and price and availability.

- *Living standards* have a known effect on the propensity to fly. Countries on a growth curve up to approximately US$20,000 per capita see correspondingly faster increases in the number of flights taken per person per year.
- *Population and demographics* reflects not just population trends over the next 20 years but also measures such as the old-age dependency ratio. On these measures, countries such as Japan, Russia, and Ukraine are expected to undergo significant population decline. African nations, on the other hand, are set for rapid population growth. Typically, nations with growing populations also have younger populations, and working-age groups are more likely to fly than those over 65.
- *Price and availability* of airline services also impact extent of future air connectivity. The unit cost of air transport has fallen by a factor of four since 1950. However, the past decade has seen prices bottom out, largely due to the increased cost of oil. In the coming two decades, the downward trend in the real cost of air travel is expected to resume, at a rate of around 1 to 1.5 percent per year. Air connectivity is expected to increase with the addition of new longer-range mid-size aircraft. Greater liberalization of air markets has the potential to increase global air traffic growth by over one percentage point per year.[1]

In fact, the Asia-Pacific share of the global middle class was 28 percent in 2009, and is forecast to reach 54 percent by 2020. An expected surge in the number of Chinese tourists represents one of the industry's greatest opportunities; according to some estimates, China outbound travel will double in the next five to seven years.[2] Even in Africa, a group of new-generation carriers led by Equatorial Congo Airlines (ECAir) is trying to shake off that continent's image as one of unsafe, unreliable, and unsustainable air transport[3] in anticipation of increased demand.

Freight

After two years of either flat or slightly negative traffic growth, demand for air cargo transport began to grow slowly and steadily during the second quarter of 2013. The uptick in traffic continued into the second half to end the year 0.9 percent above the 2012 traffic total. Growth continued to gather strength in 2014, nearly recovering the long-term trend rate. World air cargo traffic is forecast to grow an average 4.7 percent per year over the next 20 years to reach a total of more than twice the number of revenue ton–kilometers (RTK) logged in 2013. The number of airplanes in the freighter fleet will increase by more than half by the end of the same period.[4] Asia will continue to lead the world in average annual air cargo growth, with domestic China and intra-Asia markets expanding 6.7 percent and 6.5 percent per year, respectively. The Asia–North America and Europe–Asia markets will grow slightly faster than the world average growth rate.[5]

Interestingly, competition with the maritime industry could present a challenge for air cargo. Changes in the containership industry have enticed shippers to move their freight away from air cargo when schedules and time commitments to customers permit. Containership pricing is generally 10 times cheaper per unit weight than air cargo but at the expense of longer and less reliable transit times. The goods that are shipped by air are high value, time sensitive, potentially perishable, and require speedy and reliable transport. But even these can, in some cases, be moved by sea.[6] Fresh flowers, for example, used to move exclusively by air. However, ocean transport costs can be half those of airfreight, an important consideration for price-conscious supermarkets and florists. Proponents say certain roses, carnations, and other hearty varieties show no ill effects from the sea voyages spent in refrigerated containers a degree or two above freezing.[7] To continue to compete effectively with containerships, the air cargo industry must ensure that the service benefits of air transportation are not eroded. For example, track-and-trace tools, once the sole provenance of the air express industry, are now commonplace among surface transport providers. Changes in the behavior of shippers have also affected the air cargo market. E-mail and the electronic transmission of documents have reduced the need to ship many types of small parcels and documents that are the life blood of express and courier companies. Better information and improved supply chain visibility allow shippers to plan and manage their supply chains with a higher degree of confidence, encroaching on one of the primary advantages of air cargo. Air cargo has traditionally offered shippers a unique means to recover from unforeseen events and emergencies.[8]

Falling Fuel Prices

The precipitous drop in oil prices is among the most significant—and unexpected—forces in the global economy today. Thanks to a combination of increased production (especially in the United States) and muted demand, the spot price of West Texas Intermediate crude fell from $109 in July 2014 to $45 in January 2015, and has since rebounded to above $50. Airlines stand to gain the most from reduced prices in several ways. First, roughly a third of their costs are associated with fuel. Even better, carriers have yet to face direct competitive pressures to pass fuel savings on to customers. Any ticket price reductions will be driven primarily by competitive dynamics (i.e., supply and demand), rather than by reductions in fixed fuel surcharge rates. In addition, airlines now have the opportunity to rewrite their hedging contracts in order to lock in prices around $50 per barrel for the foreseeable future. Second, lower oil prices also mean increased consumer spending and a concomitant improvement in global trade. As a result, airline profitability has soared; the IATA projected early in 2014 that global airlines would reap a collective profit of $19.9 billion in 2014, and $25.0 billion in 2015. A third benefit, of more interest to passengers, is that break-even load factors will fall, making flights profitable with fewer filled seats, thus raising the possibility that the empty middle seat could return. Fourth, the value of older aircraft currently in service rises with lower fuel costs. As noted in a previous chapter, some airlines are already extending the use of older aircraft they may otherwise have disposed of. At the same time, cheaper oil pushes up the relative cost of acquiring new fuel-efficient aircraft, such as the Boeing 787. While a longer-term trend away from fuel-efficient aircraft is unlikely, depressed oil prices could allow airlines to take advantage of an older fleet as long as lower prices persist. Finally, an extended period of higher margins could also unlock capital for investment. Airlines that have recently been cash constrained could push to modernize their fleets—a trend that could be particularly viable for airlines in developing countries. Alternatively, airlines can invest in an improved customer experience to help differentiate themselves from their competitors. Some potential options include terminal modernizations and aircraft interior upgrades in seats and entertainment systems.[9]

Challenges

Infrastructure

One of the most serious long-term issues facing the airline industry, especially in the United States, is a woefully inadequate system of airports and airways tied together by an antiquated air traffic control system.

Airports

Many of today's airports are operating on the sites where they were first constructed decades ago. Unfortunately, many of these locations, which were away from populated areas when the facilities were built, have been surrounded by development in the ensuing years such that expansion is virtually impossible. A planned revamping of terminal facilities at La Guardia Airport (LGA) in New York is highlighting the problem. LGA opened in 1939, and has long been among the most congested U.S. airports. In the 12 months through June 2015, about 27 percent of arriving flights were at least 15 minutes late, the third worse rate among the top 30 U.S. airports behind San Francisco and Chicago O'Hare. About 22 percent of departing flights in the same period were at least 15 minutes late. Perhaps more importantly, the airport had nearly seven tarmac delays of at least an hour for every 1,000 flights in 2014, the highest rate in the United States.

The two biggest challenges for improving La Guardia's punctuality and efficiency are airspace congestion and runway capacity, issues the redesign does not address.[10] San Francisco's situation is very similar to La Guardia's as both have bodies of water on one side, major highways on another, and commercial development or residential neighborhoods in extremely close proximity. Essentially, runway expansion for both is virtually impossible. A similar situation exists in Chicago. In 2000, O'Hare and Midway airports reached operational capacity; yet, to date, nothing has been done to remedy the problem as the city vacillates between adding another runway at O'Hare, and building another airport known as the South Suburban Airport in Peotone, Illinois, south of Chicago.[11] So far, no decision has been made, even though United and American Airlines have shifted much of their domestic hub operations away from O'Hare to Denver and Dallas, respectively. Furthermore, O'Hare's cargo ranking has dropped from 12th in the world in 2001 to 21st today.[12]

Even in situations where the land is available, expansion can be extremely problematic. Area residents, some of whom may be displaced by the project, object to the noise and environmental damage that can come both with the construction and the finished facility. The development of Narita Airport in Tokyo in the 1970s was an unfortunate case in point. The Japanese government originally tried to buy the necessary land in the area with the agreement of landowners. However, when a significant number of landowners refused to sell, the government decided in 1971 to forcefully evict the residents in the area, which is legal by Japanese law. This action led to frequent and often violent clashes involving thousands of protesters and riot police, the destruction of costly equipment in the airport control tower and, ultimately, loss of life. These efforts were massively successful in getting the opening of the airport delayed; the original plans were to open the airport in the early 1970s but Narita finally opened on the 20th of May, 1978.[13] More recently, protests continue in Frankfurt against the level of aircraft noise brought on by the opening of the fourth runway in 2011.[14] In addition, more than 20 flights were canceled on July 13, 2015, at Heathrow Airport in London after members of an environmental group cut through a perimeter fence and chained themselves to one another on a runway to protest against the possible construction of a third runway at the airport.[15] The only real solution is to build airports away from people, for example, in the middle of nowhere. Osaka's Kansai International Airport was located on a man-made island in Osaka Bay, 40 kilometers the city.[16] Hong Kong's Chek Lap Kok airport opened in July of 1998, also on a largely man-made island, 33 kilometers from downtown.[17] Even Denver International Airport, the only major facility to be built in the United States in the last 25 years, is located 23 miles northeast of downtown Denver, replacing Stapleton Airport that was only six miles away.[18] Unfortunately, the farther away the airport from the city it supports, the greater the ground access challenges for passengers.

The reality, however, is that airports worldwide are facing the need for more runways. Hong Kong is already planning to add one to its relatively new facility, with construction to start in 2016. Seoul's Incheon Airport will construct a fourth and fifth runway beginning in 2020; Singapore Changi will convert a military runway into a third commercial runway in 2020, the same year Guangzhou Baiyun will build a fourth and fifth runway. Shanghai Pudong will add a fifth runway in 2017 and Shenzhen Bao'an will begin work on a third runway in 2018. Rightly or wrongly, these cities are in nations where social concerns often take a back seat to economic development. Contrast this situation to that discussed previously regarding Heathrow. The debate over where to build a new runway in Southeast England (Heathrow or Gatwick) has been ongoing for 25 years, with no real resolution in sight. In contrast to those Asian airports discussed earlier, the main opposition in Britain is coming from residential concerns.[19]

Air Traffic Control Systems

Like safety oversight, air traffic control is very much a national responsibility. As noted in an earlier chapter, the United States air traffic control system, widely regarded as safe but outmoded, is built, maintained, and staffed by the federal government. In 2003, Congress mandated that Federal Aviation Administration (FAA) create a plan to implement the Next Generation Air Transportation System (NextGen) that would shift from the present ground-based air traffic management system to a more effective satellite-based one that would be cost effective and reduce flight delays that were anticipated to only get worse as traffic increased. Originally envisioned as a two-decade long project, this effort includes several components, such as:

- Redesigning airspace and deploying new performance-based flight procedures
- Developing systems to help controllers better manage air traffic
- Providing critical technologies and infrastructure for NextGen[20]

Specifically, there are eight fundamental capabilities that will be provided by NextGen:

- Network-enabled information systems
- Performance-based operations and services
- Weather assimilated into decision making
- Layered, adaptive security
- Positioning, navigation, and timing services
- Aircraft trajectory-based operations
- Equivalent visual operations
- Super-density arrival and departure operations[21]

Clearly, NextGen is a huge, expensive (estimated at $40 billion for the government and system users), and complex undertaking. As an alternative, some members of Congress suggest the United States should follow the lead of the more than four dozen other nations, from Australia to the UK, that have already adopted some type of privatization for their previously state-run navigation services. Advocates of this view say a down-sized FAA would retain authority over safety and regulation as national authorities have done in those other countries. Canada's government spun off its system, which funds services through user fees, in 1996. While that system, called Nav Canada, handles far fewer flights than the United States, some in the industry see it as a model. Nav Canada receives no federal funding but can sell bonds against its revenue stream and has been able to significantly upgrade its systems and even sell its own technology solutions to other air navigation providers. However, the sheer volume of flights handled in the United States, approximately 75,000 per day, makes any kind of change a difficult one. The most aggressive proponents of privatization say that a new structure could assure more reliable funding, via fees that airspace users would pay, than the current mix of congressional appropriations and a hodgepodge of taxes. Such a change could help advance the FAA's troubled NextGen air traffic modernization drive, widely criticized by government watchdogs and air-space users for delays and for being over budget and ineffective.[22]

Eurocontrol, the European Organization for the Safety of Air Navigation, is similar to the United States in that it is an intergovernmental organization with 41 Member States, committed to building, together with its partners, a Single European Sky that will deliver safe, efficient, and environmentally friendly air traffic operations throughout the European region.[23]

Unfortunately, air traffic control services are much less sophisticated in other parts of the world, most notably throughout Africa. For example, conditions at Camp Lemonnier in Djibouti, the base for U.S. pilots flying sensitive missions over Yemen and Somalia, have become so dire that American warplanes and civilian airliners alike are routinely placed in jeopardy. (Camp Lemonnier shares its two runways with Djibouti's only international airport, a French military base, and a small contingent of Japanese military aircraft.) Military documents, based on observation reports from the flight tower, describe scenes that would be comical if not for the potential for disaster. Some controllers habitually dozed on the floor while on duty, pulling a blanket over their heads to drown out radio traffic. Others immersed themselves in video games and personal phone calls while ignoring communication from pilots. Still others punished American flight crews for a perceived lack of respect by forcing them to circle overhead until they ran low on fuel. A common vice in the flight tower was chewing *khat*, a leafy plant that acts as a stimulant and is banned in the United States but legal and popular in Djibouti, according to the documents. Outsiders who tried to impose order did so at their peril. One Djiboutian supervisor was beaten up by a controller and tossed down the flight tower stairs. A U.S. Navy officer was threatened with a pipe. The documents chronicle an ill-fated $7 million

U.S. program in which former FAA officials were tapped to retrain the Djiboutian air traffic controllers in 2012 and 2013. The effort collapsed after the Djiboutians stopped showing up for classes and locked the American trainers out of the flight tower.[24] In another example, in 2007, a new Kenya Airways Boeing 737-800 crashed into a Cameroon mangrove swamp after a midnight departure in bad weather at Douala, killing all 114 passengers and crew. The wreckage of the 737 lay undiscovered for two days, barely five kilometers from an international airport without any radar system and where no one had noticed that the Kenya Airways pilots had fallen silent less than two minutes after their takeoff.[25]

Dealing with Prosperity

U.S. airlines have benefitted from years of restructuring and consolidation, a tighter focus by management on profitability, and a roughly 55 percent drop since mid-2014 in the price of oil, which has gone from the industry's biggest cost to its second after labor. Earnings collectively topped $8 billion in the first half of 2015 alone, providing funds for repairing balance sheets and investing in their products. Finally, planes are fuller than ever. Unfortunately for management, these improvements are not going unnoticed. Airline workers are aggressively pursuing salary increases after years of wage reductions and layoffs. As the number of airlines has shrunk to the point where 80 percent of domestic traffic is served by just four carriers, those that remain find themselves under increasing government scrutiny for such things as alleged price gouging and collusion.[26] Finally, industry concerns are growing that growth plans have been too ambitious, which could lead to overcapacity and price wars. This trend could become even more extreme if two factors change. First, Airbus and Boeing are both considering further narrow body product increases beyond what they have already announced. Second, as was mentioned earlier in this chapter, falling fuel prices could lead carriers to retain older aircraft that had been scheduled for retirement.[27]

Global Competitive Environment

As has been repeatedly emphasized throughout this book, the global aviation landscape is constantly changing. Low-cost carriers (LCCs) that began by providing localized services are eager to expand into long-haul markets. Carriers from the United States and Europe that have historically dominated the global aviation industry are being supplanted by competitors from the Middle East and Asia who are increasingly challenging these airlines in their home markets, a process that will be exacerbated by the gradual weakening of cabotage laws. Deregulation will continue as will the proliferation of new airlines in all parts of the world. Competition, in short, will only increase.

Service Quality Issues

Because airlines are a service industry, the Service Quality Model depicted in Figure 6.1 is useful in illustrating how customer dissatisfaction can develop. Ignoring the arrows, the model represents the basic marketing

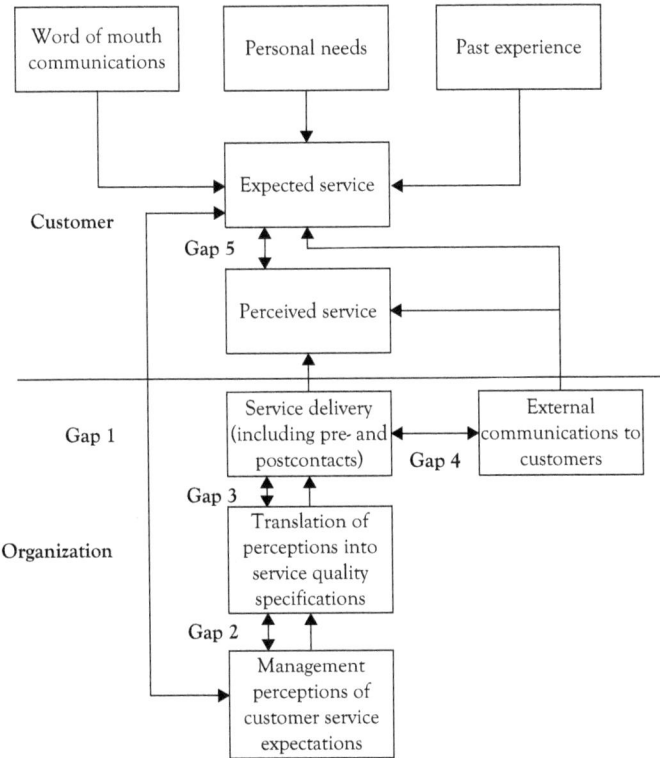

Figure 6.1 Service quality model

Source: Zeithaml, Berry, and Parasuraman.[28]

process. That is, the chart is divided into two parts: customers are on the top, management on the bottom. Managers must first learn what customers expect in terms of service. Once management understands its customers' needs, it can put together a service mix that will satisfy them. The customer benefits offered by the firm must be communicated to the buyers so that they understand why the firm provides more value than a competitor. That value must then be delivered to the customer in a way that meets his expectations. If the service the buyer receives meets his expectations, then he will be satisfied and the firm will profit. The arrows, or Service Quality Gaps, depicted in the model represent potential sources of customer dissatisfaction. Each of these Gaps will be explained in the following.

Gap 1

Gap 1 illustrates the situation when management does not really understand its customers' needs. For example, managers might assume that passengers desire an in-flight amenity which, in fact, they do not. Either insufficient market research has been performed or the results have been misinterpreted. Whatever the reason, management cannot hope to design and deliver quality service if it does not completely understand what its customers want.

Gap 2

Gap 2 opens when management does know what its customers desire (i.e., Gap 1 does not exist) but is unwilling or unable to satisfy their needs. Perhaps customer expectations are too high or the firm simply lacks the resources to adequately meet them. Alternatively, customers may not be sufficiently aware of their "true" travel needs so that their stated desires are inconsistent with their actual requirements. Again, the service mix developed and offered to customers does not meet their expectations, and this results in dissatisfaction.

Gap 3

Gap 3 is an especially troubling one because it signifies the situation where managers know what customers want and have developed a high-value offering to meet those needs, but that service is poorly delivered.

For example, the passenger may be satisfied with the airline's reservation and ticketing process, but the gate agent is rude and refuses to change a seat assignment. Thus, the customer is dissatisfied with the whole encounter (Gap 5). Often the difficulty is that the only carrier employee the passenger comes into contact with is the flight attendant, ticket agent, or customer service representative. If this person is upset for some reason or simply disinterested, he or she can undermine all of management's best efforts to provide quality service.

Gap 4

Gap 4 is created when the organization promises something to the customer that is subsequently not provided. For example, the airline promises that passengers will receive their checked bags once the aircraft arrives at the destination airport. Unfortunately, for a variety of reasons, bags are misrouted or lost, and do not arrive with the customer. While most people are reunited with their luggage relatively quickly, passenger resentment for this situation has increased with the arrival of baggage fees, which are typically not refunded when a bag is mishandled, leading to customer dissatisfaction (Gap 5).

Gap 5

Gap 5 is the most critical opening, because it reflects a situation in which the service received by customers is different than what they expected. The buyer is dissatisfied because his actual experience was less than what he anticipated. On the other hand, the customer may actually experience better service than what he was prepared for, but this situation presents its own challenges and is beyond the scope of this paper. Gap 5 also results when any of the other four Gaps open. However, Gap 5 may also open by itself. Note that satisfactory performance results from the interaction of factors that the managers can control (the interior layout of the aircraft, employees) and those that they cannot (other customers, the passenger's emotional state). Thus, a customer flying on a crowded, noisy airplane may be unhappy with the experience even if the service is fine. Similarly, a person who is unhappy, irritated, or simply having a bad day may be disposed to find fault with very minor company mistakes.

External forces (i.e., laws, governmental regulations, weather) can also have an impact on the level of service provided by an airline. For example, winter weather can disrupt flight operations and strand passengers, sometimes for days. In addition, air traffic control requirements can adversely impact airline performance as well. Naturally, situations such as these can have a detrimental impact on customer service even though the company has no control over the factors causing them. The challenge for managers is to minimize the size and occurrence of service quality gaps by understanding the needs of customers, providing a service mix that meets those needs better than the competition, and constantly monitoring customer satisfaction so that corrective action can be taken immediately if required.

Based on the financial information presented earlier, U.S. airlines are doing better than they have in years. Flight reductions have led to higher load factors, fares are rising, and ancillary fees are proving to be especially lucrative. As a result, profits are up. However, none of these factors are particularly appealing from the passenger's point of view implying less schedule choices, more crowded airplanes, and higher costs. In fact, complaints filed by customers with the U.S. Department of Transportation (DOT) against U.S. carriers are up almost 70 percent for the month of June 2015 (1,566) versus the same period in 2014 (1,090).[29] When viewed in the context of the Service Quality Model, this rising level of customer dissatisfaction represents a widening of Gap 5 resulting from Gap 2: managers know their actions are unpopular with customers, but business realities require that these steps be taken anyway. What, if anything, should management do to mitigate Gap 5 and improve overall customer satisfaction?

Maintain the Status Quo

Perhaps no management action needs to be taken. Load factors are up, operating costs are down, and profitability is increasing for the first time in years. As a result, management may see a modest increase in the number of customer complaints as a small price to pay for continuing a business model that is both sustainable and profitable. A recent study found that market concentration moderates the relationship between satisfaction and profitability for the U.S. airlines. Carriers that operate in concentrated markets have fewer incentives to satisfy their customers than those that serve more competitive market.[30] The latest round of industry consolidation means customer alternatives are reduced to a smaller number of airlines all following similar strategies, so there is little incentive for passengers to switch carriers. The end result of these changes is that market power has shifted from customers back to managers, with all that change implies.

Realign Carrier Customer Service to Fit Today's Environment

There are some steps management could take to enhance the overall customer experience. First, the collection of fees must be streamlined to eliminate the passenger perception that they are being nickeled-and-dimed to death. The reality is that customers find some fees reasonable (priority boarding, preferred seating, upgrades, and Wi-Fi) while viewing others (checked baggage) as just the opposite.[31] Airlines should consider rebundling some charges into a passenger service fee that everyone pays, similar to what hotels have instituted in the form of a resort fee to cover telephone, Internet, fitness center, and so on. For an airline, such a fee could cover one checked bag, entertainment, snacks, perhaps Internet, but every passenger would pay the fee. There would probably be initial customer dissatisfaction, but the managers could mitigate this resistance by offering enough bundled value that passengers felt like they were getting something even without checking a bag. Furthermore, the presence of a relatively fixed fee would eliminate uncertainty and the feeling of constantly being asked to pay for something. Resort fees that are transparent and fully disclosed prior to check-in have been accepted by customers as preferable to multiple charges for individual items. The airlines could find the same thing happens with a passenger service fee.

Second, baggage simply must be managed better. The implementation of fees for checked luggage forced more bags into the cabin, slowing both the security screening and aircraft loading processes. If everyone paid the passenger service fee as discussed earlier, perhaps the amount and size of carry-on items would decrease. While the company might experience an increase in the quantity of checked bags, it, along with most airports, already has the infrastructure in place to absorb them. In addition, size and weight limits for cabin bags need to be enforced prior to boarding and preferably before security.

Third, fare transparency should be improved. Vague explanations regarding surcharges, taxes, and fees need to be eliminated in favor of full disclosure regarding the true cost of a ticket. Spirit Airlines was sued in August 2012 for collecting a passenger usage fee ranging from $9 to $17 per flight segment that appeared to be an officially imposed charge but was, according to the lawsuit, a scheme to collect more money from passengers while advertising a low base fare.[32] Surcharges are especially worrisome because they are intended to be temporary and typically are applied by the carrier. In theory, these should decline or disappear altogether once they are no longer needed to deal with a specific situation. In the absence of clarity, the risk to the customer is that these charges become permanent.

Finally, a system should be developed to allow for the immediate onboard reporting of passenger service-related aircraft problems. As flights are reduced and older aircraft are retired, those that remain are flying more. For example, an aircraft might depart from Atlanta for a flight to Amsterdam where it stays for a few hours before flying on to New Delhi. After turning around there, it returns to Amsterdam before continuing back to Atlanta where it is turned back around to make the same circuit again. A passenger confronted with a reading light that does not work, a seat that does not recline, or worst of all, a defective entertainment system, is likely to be stuck with that situation for the duration of their flight because higher load factors mean less opportunity to change seats. The passenger might advise a flight attendant of the deficiency, but, realistically speaking, there is really nothing the attendant can do other than document the issue in the hope that it will be taken care of at some point. Given the short turn-around times and the lack of comprehensive maintenance support available at en-route stops, the likelihood is that multiple passengers will be dissatisfied as a result of what should be a relatively minor problem. If the aircraft is turned as quickly at its domestic domicile (where maintenance activities are presumably concentrated), the problem may remain unresolved for a lengthy period of time, resulting in a number of dissatisfied customers. Given the prevalence and sophistication of in-flight entertainment systems, passengers should be able to register seat-specific complaints that can be (a) viewed immediately by flight service personnel in case there is something they can do to remedy the problem, and (b) sent via aircraft systems directly to maintenance personnel on the ground if in-flight correction is impossible.

Conclusions

The world's airlines are simultaneously facing great opportunities and fierce threats which, arguably, has been the case since the beginning of commercial aviation. As always, the task for management is to exploit the opportunities that make sense while dealing with the challenges and satisfying its customers such that the firm remains profitable. The firms that manage to do what seems impossible will succeed; those that do not will fail. In the past, carriers could rely on, to at least some extent, their governments to bail them out of trouble, but that is increasingly not the case. Within a constantly changing environment, managers must understand their customers' needs and wants, and be able to satisfy them better than the competition if the airline is to prosper and grow.

Notes

Chapter 1

1. Lee (1984, 84).
2. Lee (1984, 80).
3. Boyne (n.d.).
4. KLM (n.d.).
5. Lee (1984, 82).
6. Lee (1984, 81).
7. Lee (1984, 83).
8. Lee (1984, 101).
9. Century of Flight (n.d.).
10. Davies (1987, 12).
11. Davies (1987, 30).
12. Davies (1987, 31).
13. Davies (1987, 38).
14. America by Air (n.d.).
15. Convention on International Civil Aviation (1944).
16. Air Mobility Command (2014).
17. Kochneff (2004).
18. Peterson (2014).
19. Fundinguniverse (n.d.).
20. Laker Airways (n.d.).
21. United States General Accounting Office Report (1996, 5).
22. Poole and Butler (1991, 45).
23. "Interesting Defunct United States Airlines" (2008).
24. Jordan (2005, 9–12).
25. TSA (n.d.).
26. IATA (2015a).
27. U.S. Department of Transportation (n.d.).
28. "Cheaper Fuel Leads to Record Profits at Airlines" (2014).

29. Centre for Aviation (2011).
30. Trefis Team (2014).
31. "Largest Airlines Report Smaller Net Loss in 4th Quarter of 2012" (2013).
32. "4th-Quarter and Annual 2013 Airline Financial Data" (2014).
33. Maxon (2014).
34. Jones (2013).
35. Delta Flight Museum (n.d.).
36. N.B. (2013).
37. McLaughlin and Zajac (2014).

Chapter 2

1. The Department of Infrastructure and Regional Development (n.d.).
2. International Civil Aviation Organization (n.d.).
3. Szakal (2013).
4. The Department of Infrastructure and Regional Development (n.d.).
5. U.S. Department of State (1998).
6. U.S. Department of Transportation (n.d.).
7. U.S. Department of Transportation (n.d.).
8. Eurofound (2005).
9. Nations Online (n.d.).
10. "Annex A List of Air Carriers Which Are Banned ...." (n.d.).
11. "Airlines Black List" (n.d.).
12. Skytrax (n.d.).
13. Perrett (2014).
14. Perrett (2014).
15. Alexander (2012).
16. Eurofound (2005).
17. Clark (2013).
18. Airline Deregulation Act of 1978 (1978).
19. Lonely Planet (n.d.).
20. Barron's Finance and Investment Dictionary (n.d.).
21. Lundgren (2012).
22. Flottau (2014a).
23. Star Alliance (n.d.).

24. Sky Team Member Airlines (n.d.).

25. Oneworld Alliance (n.d.).

26. Delta Air Lines (n.d.).

27. Schmidt (1998).

28. Woellert (1998).

29. Morrell (2005).

30. Vossoughi (2013).

31. Flottau (2014b).

32. Flottau (2014b).

33. Centre for Aviation (2014).

34. Schofield (2014).

35. Schofield (2014).

36. O'Halloran (2014).

37. European Commission (2014).

38. Wadsworth (2013).

39. Castillo and Clark (2014).

40. Ostrower and Carey (2014).

41. Krantz (2014).

42. Von Hooser (2014).

43. Witkin (1989).

44. Bever (2014).

45. Wiltgen (2014).

46. Aeroflot (n.d.).

47. Vyas (2014).

48. Mahtani and Raghuvanshi (2014).

49. Kelly (2014).

Chapter 3

1. U.S. Certificated Air Carriers (n.d.).

2. U.S. Air Carriers (n.d.).

3. *The Economist* (2015).

4. Logan (2015a).

5. Logan (2015b).

6. *Huffington Post* (2014).

7. *ChinaDaily* (2014).

8. Rothman and Kernel (2014).

9. Wilson (2014).

10. Antonov (n.d.).

11. Strategy Page (2010).

12. Menchaca (2008).

13. Air America (n.d.).

14. McCartan (2009).

15. CNN News (2015).

16. Midwest Airlines (n.d.).

17. NetJets (n.d.).

18. Skjong (n.d)

19. Michaels and Wall (2015).

20. PWC (n.d.).

21. Newhouse (1982, 3).

22. Learning Curve Calculator (n.d.).

23. BBC News (2005).

24. Shankland (2014).

25. Flottau (2015a).

26. Wall (2015).

27. Supersonic Transport (n.d.).

28. "Concorde Services to End in October" (2003).

29. Carey (2012).

30. Boeing Commercial Airplanes (n.d.).

31. Carey (2012); Boeing Commercial Airplanes (n.d.).

Chapter 4

1. Read (2015).

2. Schuler (2010).

3. Marnell (1986).

4. Bisaria (2015).

5. Greenspan (2013).

6. 9/11 Attacks (2001).

7. Traveler 24 (2015).

8. Webb (2015).

9. Culbertson (2015).

10. Hall and Calderwood (2015).

11. Gardiner (2015).

12. Aviation Security (n.d.).

13. Anthony (2014).

14. This Day in History (1983).

15. Fisher (2013).

16. IATA (2015b, 2).

17. Pearce (2009).

18. Rogers (2012).

19. Office of Inspector General (2012, 2).

20. Office of Inspector General (2012, 5).

21. IATA (2015b, 1).

22. Wall and Ostrower (2015, B6).

23. Jones (2015, B1).

24. CNNMoney (2015).

25. U.S. Department of Transportation (n.d.).

26. IATA (2015b, 4).

27. Summarized from Snyder (2011).

28. The Mercatus Energy Pipeline (2015).

29. Helman (2015).

30. Maxon (2014).

31. IATA Economics Briefing No. 10 (2013).

32. Federal Aviation Administration (n.d.).

Chapter 5

1. Butcher (n.d.).

2. Farmer (2008).

3. Nicas, Brent, and Carey (2015).

4. Homeland Security (n.d.).

5. "Who Joined DHS" (n.d.).

6. Elias (2014).

7. Elias (2014).

8. Federal Air Marshalls (n.d.).

9. Griffin, Johnston, and Schwarzschild (2008).

10. Frank (2010).

11. State Sponsors of Terrorism (n.d.).

12. State Sponsors of Terrorism (n.d.).

13. Fear of Flying (n.d.).

14. EL AL Israel Airline (n.d.).

15. McKee (n.d.).

16. McKee (n.d.).

17. International Civil Aviation Organization (n.d.).

18. International Civil Aviation Organization (n.d.).

19. International Aviation Safety Assessment Program (n.d.).

20. Federal Aviation Administration (n.d.).

21. Federal Aviation Administration (n.d.).

22. Federal Aviation Administration (n.d.).

23. Mobility and Transport (n.d.).

24. Science Daily (2010).

25. Federal Aviation Administration (2015).

26. European Union Emission Trading Scheme (n.d.).

27. National Business Aviation Association (2014).

28. Airlines for America (2014).

29. Airports for the Future (2015).

30. Zhang (2010).

31. ACI Europe (n.d.).

32. Edwards and Poole (2010).

Chapter 6

1. International Air Transport Association (2014).

2. Schofield (2015, 40).

3. Buyck (2015, 34).

4. World Air Cargo Forecast 2014–2015 (2014, 1).

5. World Air Cargo Forecast 2014–2015 (2014, 3).

6. World Air Cargo Forecast 2014–2015 (2014, 8).

7. Sechler (2013).

8. World Air Cargo Forecast 2014–2015 (2014, 11).

9. Tipping, Schmahl, and Duiven (2015).

10. Nicas and Carey (2015).

11. Kelly (2015).

12. Kelly (2015).
13. Narita Airport's Troubled Past (2014).
14. Airport Watch (2015).
15. Bilefsky (2015).
16. Kansai International Airport (2015).
17. Key Dates & Events (n.d.).
18. Fast Facts—Research Center (n.d.).
19. "Runway Fever" (2015).
20. FAA's Progress and Challenges in Advancing the Next Generation Air Transportation System" (2013).
21. Trani (2008).
22. Pasztor and Carey (2015).
23. Eurocontrol (n.d.).
24. Whitlock (2015).
25. Rosthorn (n.d.).
26. Carey (2015).
27. Flottau (2015b).
28. Zeithaml, Berry, and Parasuraman (1988).
29. U.S. Department of Transportation (2015).
30. Steven, Dong, and Dresner (2012).
31. Christie (2014).
32. Martin (2012).

References

"4th-Quarter and Annual 2013 Airline Financial Data." 2014. Retrieved August 14, 2014 from http://www.rita.dot.gov/bts/press_releases/bts022_14

9/11 Attacks. History.com. http://www.history.com/topics/9-11-attacks (accessed June 24, 2015).

ACI Europe. (n.d.). Retrieved July 27, 2015 from https://www.aci-europe.org/policy/fast-facts.html

Aeroflot. (n.d.). "Aeroflot History." Retrieved October 5, 2014 from http://www.aeroflot.com/cms/en/about/history

Air America. (n.d.). http://www.air-america.org/index.php/en/about-air-america/air-america-history

Air Mobility Command. June 25, 2014 "Civil Reserve Air Fleet." Retrieved August 5, 2014 from http://www.amc.af.mil/library/factsheets/factsheet.asp?id=234

Airline Deregulation Act of 1978. 1978. Statutes at Large, Section 102(a) 5, Volume 92.

"Airlines Black List." (n.d.). Retrieved September 6, 2014 from http://www.1001crash.com/index-page-liste_noire-lg-2.html

Airlines for America. April 3, 2014. "A4A Commends European Parliament's Vote to Extend 'Stop the Clock' on Illegal EU ETS Scheme." Retrieved July 26, 2015 from http://airlines.org/news/a4a-commends-eu-parliaments-vote-to-extend-stop-the-clock-on-illegal-eu-ets-scheme/

Airport Watch. March 1, 2015. "Noise Demonstration Blasts 80 dB Recorded Plane Noise Outside Home of Frankfurt Airport CEO or 2 Hours." Retrieved July 31, 2015 from http://www.airportwatch.org.uk/european-airports/frankfurt-airport/

Airports for the Future. 2015. Retrieved July 25, 2015 from http://airportsforthefuture.org/did-you-know/

Alexander, R. March 20, 2012. "Which Is the World's Biggest Employer?" BBC News. Retrieved September 6, 2014 from http://www.bbc.com/news/magazine-17429786

America by Air. (n.d.). "The Heyday of Propeller Airlines." Retrieved August 5, 2014 from https://airandspace.si.edu/exhibitions/america-by-air/online/heyday/heyday01.cfm

"Annex A List of Air Carriers Which Are Banned ... " (n.d.). Retrieved September 6, 2014 from http://ec.europa.eu/transport/modes/air/safety/air-ban/doc/list_en.pdf

Anthony, S. July 20, 2014. "Malaysia Airlines Flight 17 Shot Down in Ukraine: How Did They Do It? (Updates)." Extreme Tech. http://www.extremetech. com/extreme/186485-malaysia-airlines-flight-17-shot-down-in-ukraine-how-did-they-do-it (accessed June 28, 2015).

Antonov. (n.d.). "ANTONOV Airlines/Worldwide Delivery of Large-Size and Extra-Heavy Cargoes." Retrieved June 9, 2015 from http://www.antonov. com/services/antonov-airlines

Aviation Security. (n.d.). http://www.dhs.gov/aviation-security (accessed June 25, 2015).

Barron's Finance and Investment Dictionary. (n.d.). Retrieved September 7, 2014 from http://www.answers.com/topic/privatization

BBC News. January 18, 2005. "Airbus Unveils 'Superjumbo' Jet." Retrieved June 12, 2015 from http://news.bbc.co.uk/2/hi/business/4183201.stm

Bever, L. August 19, 2014. "Iceland Volcano Erupts, Prompting Red Alert for Air Traffic." Retrieved October 4, 2014 from http://www.washingtonpost.com/news/morning-mix/wp/2014/08/29/iceland-volcano-erupts-prompting-red-alert-for-air-traffic/

Bilefsky, D. 2015. "Protest on Runway Over Heathrow Airport Expansion Disrupts Flights." *The New York Times*, July 13. Retrieved July 31, 2015 from http://www.nytimes.com/2015/07/14/world/europe/protest-on-runway-over-heathrow-airport-expansion-disrupts-flights.html?_r=0

Bisaria, A. 2015. "30 Years Ago, Air India Flight 182 Was Blown to Bits, Here's Why No One Remembers It." *India Times*, June 24. Retrieved June 24, 2015 from http://www.indiatimes.com/lifestyle/self/30-years-ago-air-india-flight-182-was-blown-to-bits-here%E2%80%99s-why-no-one-remembers-it-233958.html

Boeing Commercial Airplanes. (n.d.). Boeing. http://www.boeing.com/resources/boeingdotcom/company/about_bca/pdf/boeing_commercial_backgrounder.pdf

Boyne, W.J. (n.d.). "History of Flight." Retrieved August 5, 2014 from http://www.britannica.com/EBchecked/topic/210191/history-of-flight/260584/The-first-airlines

Butcher, L. (n.d.). "Aviation, European liberalization, 1986-2002." Library House of Commons. Retrieved July 2, 2015 from www.parliment.uk

Buyck, C. 2015. "Raising the Bar." *Aviation Week and Space Technology*, August 17–30, p. 34.

Carey, S. 2012. "Delta Flies New Route to Profits: Older Jets." *The Wall Street Journal*, November 15. Retrieved June 12, 2015 from http://www.wsj.com/articles/SB10001424052970203406404578072960852910072

Carey, S. 2015. "Dark Clouds Loom for Airlines Even as Their Profits Take Off." *The Wall Street Journal*, August 19, pp. 1–2.

Castillo, M., and C. Clark. July 14, 2014. "When Civilian Planes Are Shot Down." Retrieved October 4, 2014 from http://www.cnn.com/2014/07/17/world/historyplanes-shot-down/

Centre for Aviation. 2011. "Airline Industry in Continued 'Crisis' State Amid Uncertain Outlook: IATA." http://centreforaviation.com/analysis/airline-industry-in-continued-crisis-state-amid-uncertain-outlook-iata-60122 Retrieved August 7, 2014.

Centre for Aviation. January 1, 2014. "Asia-Pacific 2014 Outlook: Faster Growth for Low-Cost Airlines as LCC Fleet Reaches 1,000 Aircraft." Retrieved October 5, 2014 from http://centreforaviation.com/analysis/asia-pacific-2014-outlook-faster-growth-for-low-cost-airlines-as-lcc-fleet-reaches-1000-aircraft-146351

Century of Flight. (n.d.). "The History of Flight." Retrieved August 5, 2014 from http://www.century-of-flight.net/index.htm

"Cheaper Fuel Leads to Record Profits at Airlines." 2014. *The New York Times*, October 23. http://www.nytimes.com/2014/10/24/business/cheaper-fuel-helps-airlines-to-record-profits.html?_r=0

ChinaDaily. September 17, 2014. "Over 14,000 Chinese Muslims Set for Mecca Pilgrimage." ChinaDaily.com. Retrieved June 8, 2015 from http://www.chinadaily.com.cn/china/2014-09/17/content_18616224.htm

Christie, L. January 29, 2014. "5 Airline Fees We Hate the Most." CNNMoney. Retrieved August 22, 2015 from http://money.cnn.com/2014/01/28/pf/hated-airline-fees/

Clark, N. 2013. "Cost Cuts Helped Air France-KLM Trim Operating Loss in 2012." *New York Times*, February 22. Retrieved September 6, 2014 from http://www.nytimes.com/2013/02/23/business/global/23iht-airfrance23.html?_r=0

CNN News. January 19, 2015. "Airbus' Beluga: Giant of the Skies Set to Get Even Large." Retrieved June 9, 2015 from http://www.cnn.com/2015/01/19/travel/airbus-new-beluga-super-transporter-plane/

CNNMoney. April 24, 2015. "Airlines Saved $3.4 Billion. You Saved 66 Cents." http://money.cnn.com/2015/04/24/news/companies/airline-fuel-savings-fares/ (accessed June 23, 2015).

"Concorde Services to End in October." April 10, 2003. CNN.com/world. Retrieved from http://www.cnn.com/2003/WORLD/europe/04/10/biz.trav.concorde/ (accessed September 10, 2015).

Convention on International Civil Aviation. December 7, 1944. Retrieved August 5, 2014 from http://www.icao.int/publications/Documents/7300_orig.pdf

Culbertson, A. 2015. "All Pilots Know Malaysia Airlines Flight MH370 NOT an Accident and WAS Hijacked." *Express*, May 10. http://www.express.co.uk/news/world/576148/All-pilots-know-Malaysia-Airlines-flight-MH370-not-accident-hijacked (accessed June 25, 2015).

Davies, R.E.G. 1987. *Pan Am: An Airline and Its Aircraft*. New York: Orion Books.

Delta Air Lines (n.d.). Retrieved September 7, 2014 from www.delta.com

Delta Flight Museum. (n.d.). Retrieved August 7, 2014 from http://www.deltamuseum.org/exhibits/delta-history/timeline/decades/2000

The Department of Infrastructure and Regional Development. (n.d.). "The Bilateral System—How International Air Services Work." Retrieved September 6, 2014 from http://www.infrastructure.gov.au/aviation/international/bilateral_system.aspx

The Economist. May 5, 2015. "Sky-High Profits." Retrieved June 11, 2015 from http://www.economist.com/blogs/gulliver/2015/05/airline-baggage-fees

Edwards, C., and R.W. Poole. June 2010. "Airports and Air Traffic Control." The CATO Institute: Downsizing the Federal Government. Retrieved July 28, 2015 from http://www.downsizinggovernment.org/transportation/airports-atc

EL AL Israel Airline. (n.d.). "Check-in Times." Retrieved July 23, 2015 from http://www.elal.com/en/PassengersInfo/Useful-Info/Airport-Services/Pages/Appearance-Time.aspx

Elias, B. March 31, 2014. "Risk-Based Approaches to Airline Passenger Screening." Congressional Research Service, p. i. Retrieved July 2, 2015 from https://www.hsdl.org/?view&did=752251

Eurocontrol. (n.d.). "Who We Are." Retrieved August 22, 2015 from https://www.eurocontrol.int/articles/who-we-are

Eurofound. September 28, 2005. "Industrial Relations in the Airline Sector." Retrieved September 6, 2014 from http://www.eurofound.europa.eu/eiro/2005/08/study/tn0508101s.htm

European Commission. May 19, 2014. "Airport Charges Directive." Retrieved September 19, 2014 from http://ec.europa.eu/transport/modes/air/airports/airport_charges_en.htm

European Union Emissions Trading Scheme. (n.d.). Retrieved July 26, 2015 from https://en.wikipedia.org/wiki/European_Union_Emission_Trading_Scheme

"FAA's Progress and Challenges in Advancing the Next Generation Air Transportation System." July 17, 2013. Statement of the Honorable Calvin L. Scovel III, Inspector General, U.S. Department of Transportation, p. 2. Retrieved August 21, 2015 from https://transportation.house.gov/uploadedfiles/documents/2013-07-17-scovel.pdf

Farmer, S.B. 2008. "The European Experience with Merger and Deregulation." In *Competition Policy and Merger Analysis in Deregulated and Newly Competitive Industries*, eds. P.C. Carstensen and S.B. Farmer, 201–204. Retrieved July 2, 2015 from http://econpapers.repec.org/bookchap/elgeechap/3791_5f9.htm

Fast Facts—Research Center. (n.d.). Retrieved August 21, 2015 from https://business.flydenver.com/info/research/facts.asp

Fear of Flying. (n.d.). "Airport Security—After 9/11." Retrieved July 24, 2015 from http://www.fearofflyinganxiety.com/airport-security/

Federal Air Marshalls. (n.d.). Retrieved July 2, 2015 from http://www.tsa.gov/about-tsa/federal-airmarshals

Federal Aviation Administration. (n.d.). "Aviation Safety (AVS)" Retrieved July 25, 2015 from http://www.faa.gov/about/office_org/headquarters_offices/avs/

Federal Aviation Administration. (n.d.). "Sustainable Alternative Jet Fuels." Retrieved June 26, 2015 from https://www.faa.gov/about/office_org/headquarters_offices/apl/research/alternative_fuels/

Federal Aviation Administration. January 2015. "Aviation Emissions, Impacts and Mitigations: A Primer." FAA Office of Environment and Energy, p. 17. Retrieved July 26, 2015 from http://www.faa.gov/regulations_policies/policy_guidance/envir_policy/media/Primer_Jan2015.pdf

Fisher, M. 2013. "The Forgotten Story of Iran Air Flight 655." *Washington Post*, October 16. http://www.washingtonpost.com/blogs/worldviews/wp/2013/10/16/the-forgotten-story-of-iran-air-flight-655/ (accessed June 28, 2015).

Flottau, J. 2014a. "Live and Don't Let Die." *Aviation Week and Space Technology*, August 25, p. 17.

Flottau, J. 2014b. "Tough Choices." *Aviation Week and Space Technology*, September 15, p. 35.

Flottau, J. 2015a. "Learning Curve." *Aviation Week & Space Technology*, June 8–21, p. 100.

Flottau, J. 2015b. "Truth and Consequences." *Aviation Week and Space Technology*, August 17–30, p. 14.

Frank, T. 2010. "TSA Lists 'Countries of Interest'; More Screening for Some Fliers." *USA Today*, January 4. Retrieved July 24, 2015 from http://usatoday30.usatoday.com/news/washington/2010-01-03-tsa-flights-screening_N.htm

Fundinguniverse. (n.d.). "Icelandair History." Retrieved August 7, 2014 from http://www.fundinguniverse.com/company-histories/icelandair-history/

Gardiner, B. June 14, 2015. "Off with Your Shoes: A Brief History of Airport Security." Wired. http://www.wired.com/2013/06/fa_planehijackings/ (accessed June 25, 2015).

Gourdin, K.N. 2013. "Extracted with Permission from the Evolving Relationship Between Airline Profitability and Passenger Satisfaction." *Journal of Transportation Management* 24, no. 1, pp. 7–21.

Greenspan, J. December 20, 2013. "Remembering the 1988 Lockerbie Bombing." History in the Headlines. www.history.com. http://www.history.com/news/remembering-the-1988-lockerbie-bombing (accessed June 24, 2015).

Griffin, D., K. Johnston, and T. Schwarzschild. March 24, 2008. "Air Marshals Missing from Almost All Flights." CNN. Retrieved July 28, 2015 from http://www.cnn.com/2008/TRAVEL/03/25/siu.air.marshals/

Hajj. 2014. "Islam's Pilgrimage to Mecca: Facts, History and Dates of the Muslim Holiday."*Huffington Post*, September 26. Retrieved June 8, 2015 from http://www.huffingtonpost.com/2014/09/26/hajj-2014_n_5889806.html

Hall, A., and I. Calderwood. 2015. "Did Killer Germanwings Pilot Change His Mind at the Last Minute? Black Box Reveals he Tried to Override Automatic Descent in Final Moments." *Daily Mail*, May 7. http://www.dailymail.co.uk/news/article-3071932/Germanwings-pilot-tried-avoid-Alps-crash-minute.html (accessed June 25, 2015).

Helman, C. 2015. "How Cheap Oil Has Delta Air Lines Jet Fooled." *Forbes*, February 9. http://www.forbes.com/sites/christopherhelman/2015/01/21/how-cheap-oil-has-delta-air-lines-jet-fooled/ (accessed June 23, 2015).

Homeland Security. (n.d.). "Creation of the Department of Homeland Security." Retrieved July 2, 2015 from http://www.dhs.gov/creation-department-homeland-security

IATA Economics Briefing No 10. June 2013. "Profitability and the Air Transport Value Chain."http://www.pwc.com/en_US/us/industrial-products/publications/assets/pwc-2014-global-airline-ceo-survey.pdf (accessed June 26, 2015).

IATA (International Air Transportation Association). 2015a. "Fact Sheet: Fuel." Retrieved August 7, 2014 from www.iata.org/pressroom/facts_figures/fact_sheets/Documents/fact-sheet-fuel.pdf

IATA. 2015b. IATA Economic Performance of the Airline Industry 2015 Mid-Year Report. http://www.iata.org/whatwedo/Documents/economics/IATA-Economic-Performance-of-the-Industry-mid-year-2015-report.pdf (accessed June 22, 2015).

"Interesting Defunct United States Airlines." November 15, 2008. Retrieved August 7, 2014 from http://www.rioleo.org/interesting-defunct-united-states-airlines.php

International Air Transport Association. October 16, 2014. "New IATA Passenger Forecast Reveals Fast-Growing Markets of the Future." International Air Transport Association. Retrieved July 29, 2015 from http://www.iata.org/pressroom/pr/pages/2014-10-16-01.aspx

International Aviation Safety Assessment Program. (n.d.). Retrieved July 25, 2015 from http://www.faa.gov/about/initiatives/iasa/media/FAA_Initiatives_IASA.pdf

International Civil Aviation Organization. (n.d.). "About ICAO." Retrieved July 24, 2015 from http://www.icao.int/about-icao/Pages/default.aspx

International Civil Aviation Organization. (n.d.). "Freedoms of the Air." Retrieved September 6, 2014 from http://www.icao.int/Pages/freedomsAir.aspx.

International Civil Aviation Organization. (n.d.). "History." Retrieved July 24, 2015 from http://www.icao.int/secretariat/TechnicalCooperation/Pages/history.aspx

Jones, C. 2013. "Airline Industry on Profitable Path." *USA Today*, October 25, 2013. Retrieved August 11, 2014 from http://www.usatoday.com/story/travel/flights/2013/10/24/airlines-profit-earnings/3177585/

Jones, C. 2015. "Air Travel Demand Forecast to Double." *USA Today*, June 10, p. B1.

Jordan, W.A. 2005. "Airline Entry Following U.S. Deregulation: The Definitive List of Startup Passenger Airlines, 1979-2003." Retrieved August 7, 2014 from http://www.trforum.org/forum/downloads/2005_Deregulation_paper.pdf

Kansai International Airport. May 5, 2015. japan-guide.com. Retrieved July 31, 2015 from http://www.japan-guide.com/e/e2033.html

Kelly, R. 2014. "Qantas Airways Takes $2.39 Billion Charge." *The Wall Street Journal*, August 29, p. B4.

Kelly, R. 2015. "Counterpoint: Still Waiting on 3rd Airport." *Chicago Sun Times*, April 12. Retrieved August 21, 2015 from http://chicago.suntimes.com/news/7/71/514180/counterpoint-2

Key Dates & Events. (n.d.). Retrieved July 31, 2015 from http://www.hongkongairport.com/eng/media/key-dates-events.html

KLM. (n.d.). "History." Retrieved August 5, 2014 from http://www.klm.com/corporate/en/about-klm/history/index.html

Kochneff, E. 2004. "The Rise and Fall of People Express." Retrieved August 5, 2014 from http://www.airliners.net/aviation-articles/read.main?id=68

Krantz, M. 2014. "Fears About Ebola Virus Spread to Travel Stocks." *USA Today*, October 2, p. 5B.

Laker Airways. (n.d.). *Wikipedia*. Retrieved August 7, 2014 http://en.wikipedia.org/wiki/Laker_Airways

"Largest Airlines Report Smaller Net Loss in 4th Quarter of 2012." 2013. Retrieved August 14, 2014 from http://www.rita.dot.gov/bts/press_releases/bts023_13

"Learning Curve Calculator." Retrieved June 15, 2015 from http://fas.org/news/reference/calc/learn.htm

Lee, D.D. 1984. "Herbert Hoover and the Development of Commercial Aviation." *The Business History Review* 58, no. 1, pp. 78–102.

Logan, J.A. January 27, 2015a. "DOT Should Reject Norwegian Air's Foreign Air Carrier Application." TheHill.com. Retrieved June 10, 2015 fromhttp://thehill.com/blogs/pundits-blog/labor/230764-dot-should-reject-norwegian-airs-foreign-air-carrier-application

Logan, G. 2015b. "Differences Between Scheduled & Charter Flights." Demand Media. Retrieved June 8, 2015 from http://traveltips.usatoday.com/differences-between-scheduled-chartered-flights-55014.html

Lonely Planet. (n.d.). Retrieved September 7, 2014 from http://www.lonelyplanet.com/sri-lanka/transport/getting-around

Lundgren, K. September 25, 2012. "EU Revives Plans to End Limits on Foreign Airline Stakes." Retrieved September 7, 2014 from http://www.bloomberg.com/news/2012-09-25/eu-revives-plans-to-end-limits-on-foreign-airline-stakes.html

Mahtani, S., and G. Raghuvanshi. 2014. "In Mynamar, the Glow from Aviation Dims." *The Wall Street Journal*, August 25, p. B7.

Marnell, J. 1986. "At the End of the Rainbow … D.B. Cooper's Parachute." *Los Angeles Times*, November 25. Retrieved June 24, 2015 from http://articles.latimes.com/keyword/d-b-cooper

Martin, H. 2012. "Lawsuit Claims Spirit Airlines Misled Passengers About Fee." *Los Angeles Times*, August 8. Retrieved August 22, 2015 from www.latimes.com

Maxon, T. 2014. "U.S. Airlines Increase Their Profits Without Ballooning Their Fleets." *The Dallas Morning News*, August 9, 2014. Retrieved August 11, 2014 from http://www.dallasnews.com/business/airline-industry/20140809-u.s.-airlines-increase-their-profits-without-ballooning-their-fleets.ece

Maxon, T. 2014. "American Airlines Dumps Its Fuel Hedges-and Saves." *The Dallas Morning News*, July 16. http://www.dallasnews.com/business/airline-industry/20140716-american-airlines-dumps-its-fuel-hedges--and-saves.ece (accessed June 24, 2015).

The Mercatus Energy Pipeline. January 13, 2015. "Airlines Alter Fuel Hedging Strategies for Low Price Environment." http://www.mercatusenergy.com/blog/bid/106187/Airlines-Alter-Fuel-Hedging-Strategies-for-Low-Price-Environment (accessed June 23, 2015).

McCartan, B. 2009. "Weapons Seizure Hits North Korea Hard." *Asia Times Online*, December 22. Retrieved June 9, 2015 from http://www.atimes.com/atimes/Southeast_Asia/KL22Ae01.html

McKee, R. (n.d.). "Top 5 El Al Security Policies and Airport Security After 9/11." Retrieved July 23, 2015 from http://www.askmen.com/top_10/travel/top-5-el-al-policies-that-would-improve-us-airline-safety.html

McLaughlin, D., and A. Zajac. April 26, 2014. "American Airlines–US Airways Merger Settlement Approved." Bloomberg. Retrieved August 7, 2014 from http://www.bloomberg.com/news/2014-04-25/american-airlines-settlement-over-us-airways-merger-approved.html

Menchaca, R. 2008. "Air Force Hires Russian Jet." *The Post and Courier*, January 5. Retrieved June 9, 2015 from http://www.postandcourier.com/article/20080105/PC1602/301059954

Michaels, D., and R. Wall. 2015. "For Global Jet Rivals, Battle Is on the Ground." *The Wall Street Journal*, June 12, p. A10.

Midwest Airlines. (n.d.). Retrieved June 9, 2015 from http://en.wikipedia.org/wiki/Midwest_Airlines

Mobility and Transport. (n.d.). "The European Aviation Safety Policy." Retrieved July 25, 2015 from http://ec.europa.eu/transport/modes/air/safety/index_en.htm

Morrell, P. September, 2005. "Airlines with Airlines: An Analysis of U.S. Network Airline Responses to Low Cost Carriers." *Journal of Air Transport Management* 11, no. 5, p. 9. Retrieved October 5, 2014 from https://dspace.lib.cranfield.ac.uk/bitstream/1826/1232/3/Airlines%20within%20Airlines%20analysis%20US%20network%20-%202005.pdf?origin=publication_detail

N.B. 2013. "Truly United?" *The Economist*, September 9, 2013. Retrieved August 7, 2014 from http://www.economist.com/blogs/gulliver/2013/09/united-continentalmerger

Narita Airport's Troubled Past. March 6, 2014. Retrieved July 31, 2015 from http://www.tofugu.com/2014/03/06/narita-airports-troubled-past/

National Business Aviation Association. February 7, 2014. "NBAA, Others Urge Foxx to Press for "Stop the Clock' Legislation Regarding EU-ETS." Retrieved July 26, 2015 from http://www.nbaa.org/ops/environment/eu-ets/

Nations Online. (n.d.). "Countries of the Third World." Retrieved September 6, 2014 from http://www.nationsonline.org/oneworld/third_world.htm

NetJets. (n.d.). Retrieved June 10, 2015 from https://www.netjets.com/Programs/NetJets-Share/

Newhouse, J. 1982. *The Sporty Game*. New York: Alfred A. Knoph, Inc.

Nicas, J., and S. Carey. 2015. "La Guardia Airport Makeover Likely Won't Ease Delays." *The Wall Street Journal*, July 29, pp. B1–B2.

Nicas, J., B. Kendall, and S. Carey. 2015. "Airlines Face Antitrust Probe." *The Wall Street Journal*, July 2, p. A1.

O'Halloran, B. September 4, 2014. US Ruling Hits Norwegian Air Shuttle's Long-Haul Plans." Retrieved September 7, 2014 from http://www.irishtimes.com/business/transport-and-tourism/us-ruling-hits-norwegian-air-shuttle-s-long-haul-plans-1.1916935

Office of Inspector General. September 4, 2012. "Aviation Industry Performance: A Review of the Aviation Industry, 2008–2011." United States Department of Transportation, p. 2. https://www.oig.dot.gov/sites/default/files/Aviation%20Industry%20Performance%5E9-24-12.pdf (accessed June 19, 2015.).

Oneworld Alliance. (n.d.). Retrieved September 7, 2014 from http://www.oneworld.com/member-airlines/overview

Ostrower, J., and S. Carey. October 1, 2014 "Ebola Case in the U.S. Gives Airline Investors the Jitters." Retrieved October 4, 2014 from http://online.wsj.com/articles/ebola-case-in-u-s-sends-jitters-through-airline-industry-1412184844

Pasztor, A., and S. Carey. 2015. "Support Builds to Redo U.S. Air-Traffic System." *The Wall Street Journal*, May 11. Retrieved August 22, 2015 from http://www.wsj.com/articles/support-builds-to-redo-u-s-air-traffic-system-1431389851

Pearce, B. 2009. "Airline Outlook Dominated by Recession Impact." Aviation Forecast 2009, International Air Transport Association (IATA). https://www.faa.gov/news/conferences_events/aviation_forecast_2009/agenda/media/brian_pearce.pdf (accessed June 19, 2015).

Perrett, B. 2014. "Good Deeds." *Aviation Week and Space Technology*, September 8, p. 30.

Peterson, B. 2014. "People Express the Sequel? The Budget Airline is Reborn." *Condé Nast Traveler*, June 5. Retrieved August 5, 2014 from http://www.cntraveler.com/stories/2014-06-05/people-express-founder-don-burr-sounds-off-on-the-revived-1980s-budget-airline

Poole, R.W., Jr., and V. Butler. 1999. "Airline Deregulation: The Unfinished Revolution." Retrieved August 5, 2014 from http://object.cato.org/sites/cato.org/files/serials/files/regulation/1999/4/airline.pdf

PWC. (n.d.). "Globalization of Aircraft Manufacturing: New Markets, New Players." pwc.com. Retrieved June 12, 2015 from http://www.pwc.com/us/en/industrial-products/commercial-aircraft-industry-future/globalization-new-markets-and-manufacturers.jhtml

Read, D. April 27, 2015. "Don't Believe Everything You Read: Lower Fuel Prices Aren't Why U.S. Airlines Are Earning Big Profits." www.forbes.com. Retrieved June 24, 2015 from http://www.forbes.com/sites/danielreed/2015/04/27/dont-believe-everything-you-read-lower-fuel-prices-arent-why-us-airlines-are-earning-big-profits/

Rogers, A. October 8, 2012. "The State of the Airline Industry." http://www.foxbusiness.com/travel/2012/10/08/state-airline-industry/ (accessed June 19, 2015).

Rosthorn, A. (n.d.). "Training for Total Control in African Skies." New Security Learning. Retrieved August 21, 2015 from http://www.newsecuritylearning.com/index.php/feature/154-training-for-total-control-in-african-skies

Rothman, A., and D. Kernel. 2014. "Airbus Pitches A380 Jumbo Role Serving Mecca's Million." *Bloomberg Business*, October 03. Retrieved June 8, 2015 from http://www.bloomberg.com/news/articles/2014-10-02/airbus-pitches-a380-jumbo-role-serving-mecca-s-millions

"Runway Fever." 2015. *Air Cargo World*, August, p. 26.

Schmidt, R.E. 1998. "Swissair Crash, but It was Delta's, Too." Retrieved September 7, 2014 from http://www.southcoasttoday.com/apps/pbcs.dll/article?AID=/19980905/NEWS/309059980

Schofield, A. 2014. "Long-Haul Logjam." *Aviation Week and Space Technology*, August 25, p. 23.

Schofield, A. 2014. "Long Haul Logjam." *Aviation Week and Space Technology*, August 25, p. 23.

Schofield, A. 2015. "Asia Access." *Aviation Week and Space Technology*, August 17–30, p. 40.

Science Daily. September 1, 2010. "Airline Passengers in Developing Countries Face 13 Times Crash Risk as US." Institute for Operations Research and the Management Sciences. Retrieved July 25, 2015 from http://www.sciencedaily.com/releases/2010/09/100901132235.htm

Sechler, B. 2013. "Fresh-Cut Flowers Shipped by Sea?" *The Wall Street Journal*, May 11. Retrieved July 29, 2015 from http://www.wsj.com/articles/SB10001424127887323687604578469301967755688

Shankland, S. July 23, 2014. "Want Major New Aircraft Designs? Wait Until 2030." cnnet.com. Retrieved June 12, 2015 from http://www.cnet.com/news/want-major-new-aircraft-designs-wait-until-2030/

Shuler, D. January 24, 2010. "A Short History of Air Hijacking." The Glittering Eye. Retrieved June 24, 2015 from http://theglitteringeye.com/a-short-history-of-air-hijacking/

Skjong, A. (n.d.). "How Much Does a Private Jet Flight Cost with NetJets?" Forbes Travel Guide, ND. Retrieved June 10, 2015 from http://www.forbestravelguide.com/partner/netjets/how-much-does-a-private-jet-flight-cost-with-netjets?preferredAttributionId=alex-skjong

Sky Team Member Airlines (n.d.). Retrieved September 7, 2014 from https://www.skyteam.com/en/About-us/Our-members/

Skytrax (n.d.). "1-Star Airline Rating." http://www.airlinequality.com/ratings/1-star-airline-ratings/

Snyder, B. March 21, 2011. "Fuel Hedging No Guarantee for Airlines." CNN.com. http://www.cnn.com/2011/TRAVEL/03/21/airlines.fuel.hedging/ (accessed June 23, 2015).

Star Alliance. (n.d.). "Travel the World with the Star Alliance Network." Retrieved September 7, 2014 from http://www.staralliance.com/en/about/member_airlines/

State Sponsors of Terrorism. (n.d.). Retrieved July 24, 2015 from http://www.state.gov/j/ct/list/c14151.htm

Steven, A.B., Y. Dong, and M. Dresner. 2012. "Linkages Between Customer Service, Customer Satisfaction and Performance in the Airline Industry: Investigation of Non-Linearities and Moderating Effects." *Transportation Research, Part E* 48, no. 4, p. 743–54.

Strategy Page. March 22, 2010. "Logistics: The Bottleneck." Retrieved June 9, 2015 from http://www.strategypage.com/htmw/htlog/20100322.aspx

Supersonic Transport. (n.d.). *Wikipedia*. Retrieved September 10, 2015 from https://en.wikipedia.org/wiki/Supersonic_transport (accessed September 10, 2015).

Szakal, A. September 2013. "Freedoms of the Air Explained." Retrieved October 5, 2014 from http://www.aviationlaw.eu/wp/wp-content/uploads/2013/09/Freedoms-of-the-AirExplained.pdf

This Day in History. September 1, 1983. "Korean Airlines Flight Shot Down by Soviet Union." History.com. http://www.history.com/this-day-in-history/korean-airlines-flight-shot-down-by-soviet-union (accessed June 28, 2015).

Tipping, A., A. Schmahl, and F. Duiven. 2015. "The Impact of Reduced Oil Prices on the Transportation Sector." *Strategy+Business*, February 18. Retrieved July 29, 2015 from http://www.strategy-usiness.com/article/00312?gko=ae404

Trani, A.A., Dr. January 8, 2008. "Analysis of Air Transportation Systems, Next Generation Air Transportation System." Presentation at Virginia Tech University. Retrieved August 22, 2015 from http://128.173.204.63/courses/nextor_sc08/Nextgen.pdf

Traveler 24. March 26, 2015. "8 Times Plane Crashes Were Caused by Pilot Suicides." http://traveller24.news24.com/News/Flights/8-times-plane-crashes-were-caused-by-pilot-suicides-20150326 (accessed June 25, 2015).

Trefis Team. Jun 20, 2014 "Airline Industry Will Have to Maintain Capacity Discipline to Remain Profitable." Retrieved August 7, 2014 from http://www.forbes.com/sites/greatspeculations/2014/06/20/airline-industry-will-have-tomaintain-capacity-discipline-to-remain-profitable/

TSA (Transportation Security Administration) (n.d.). AllGov.com. http://www.allgov.com/departments/department-of-homeland-security/transportation-security-administration-tsa?agencyid=7350

U.S. Air Carriers. (n.d.). Transportation.gov. Retrieved June 10, 2015 from http://www.transportation.gov/policy/aviationpolicy/licensing/US-carriers

U.S. Certificated Air Carriers. (n.d.). Retrieved June 10, 2015 from http://www.transportation.gov/sites/dot.gov/files/docs/Certificated%20Air%20Carrier%20List.pdf

U.S. Department of State. March 14, 1998. "Memorandum of Understanding Between the Government of Japan and the Government of the United States of America." http://www.state.gov/e/eb/rls/othr/ata/j/ja/114175.htm

U.S. Department of Transportation. (n.d.). "Air Service Agreements." Retrieved September 6, 2014 from http://www.dot.gov/policy/aviation-policy/international-relations/air-service-agreements

U.S. Department of Transportation. (n.d.). "Airline Fuel Cost and Consumption (U.S. Carriers-All), January 2000-April 2015." Bureau of Transportation Statistics. http://www.transtats.bts.gov/fuel.asp?pn=1 (accessed June 23, 2015).

U.S. Department of Transportation. August 2015. Air Travel Consumer Report. Retrieved August 21, 2015 from htps://www.transportation.gov/sites/dot.gov/files/docs/2015AugustATCR_1.pdf.

United States General Accounting Office Report. 1996. "Airline Deregulation: Changes in Airfares, Service, and Safety at Small, Medium-Sized, and Large Communities." Retrieved August 5, 2014 from http://www.gao.gov/assets/160/155424.pdf

Von Hooser, T. August 21, 2014. "Iceland Awaits Barðarbunga Volcano Eruption and Climatic Impact." Retrieved October 4, 2014 from http://guardianlv.com/2014/08/iceland-awaits-bardarbunga-volcano-eruption-and-climatic-impact/

Vossoughi, S. September 9, 2013. "A Company's Culture Has to Come from Within or It Will Fail." Retrieved October 5, 2014 from http://www.theglobeandmail.com/report-on-business/careers/management/a-companys-culture-has-to-come-from-within-or-it-will-fail/article14169921/?page=all

Vyas, K. 2014. "Airlines Abandon Venezuela, Stranding Fliers." *The Wall Street Journal*, August 28, p. B1.

Wadsworth, E. March 21, 2013. "DOT May Prohibit Some Alitalia Flights Due to Italy's Airport User Fees." Retrieved September 19, 2014 from http://www.aviationlawadvisor.com/2013/03/21/dot-may-prohibit-some-alitalia-flights-due-to-italys-airport-user-fees/

Wall, R. January 13, 2015. "Airbus Racks Up More 2014 Jet Orders than Boeing." wsj.com. Retrieved June 12, 2015 from http://www.wsj.com/articles/airbus-racks-up-more-2014-jet-orders-than-boeing-1421142005

Wall, R., and J. Ostrower. June 19, 2015. "Airbus, Boeing Book $107 Billion in Deals." *The Wall Street Journal* 265, no. 142, p. B6.

Webb, S. 30 July 2015. "MH370, Live News and Updates as Debris Found on Reunion Island." Mirror Website. http://www.mirror.co.uk/news/world-news/mh370-live-news-updates-debris-6162708 (accessed August 23, 2015).

Whitlock, C. 2015. "Chaos in Tower, Danger in Skies at Base in Africa." *The Washington Post*, April 30. Retrieved August 21, 2015 from https://www.washingtonpost.com/world/national-security/miscues-at-us-counterterrorism-base-put-aircraft-in-danger-documents-show/2015/04/30/39038d5a-e9bb-11e4-9a6a-c1ab95a0600b_story.html

"Who Joined DHS." (n.d.). Retrieved July 2, 2015 from http://www.dhs.gov/who-joined-dhs

Wilson, D. October 02, 2014. "FedEx, Others Get $545M in DOD Airlift Services Contracts." Law360. Retrieved June 8, 2015 from http://www.law360.com/articles/583517/fedex-others-get-545m-in-dod-airlift-services-contracts

Wiltgen, N. September 16. 2014. "Hurricane Odile Timeline: Unprecedented Cyclone Leaves Widespread Damage in Cabo San Lucas, Baja California." Retrieved October 4, 2014 from http://www.weather.com/news/weather-hurricanes/hurricane-odile-update-cabo-san-lucas-20140914

Witkin, R. December 16, 1989. "Jet Lands Safely After Engines Stop in Flight Through Volcanic Ash." Retrieved October 4, 2014 from http://www.nytimes.com/1989/12/16/us/jet-lands-safely-after-engines-stop-in-flight-through-volcanic-ash.html

Woellert, L. 1998. "Commentary: U.S. Airlines: Make Sure Your Partner's Are Safe." Retrieved September 7, 2014 from http://www.businessweek.com/stories/1998-10-18/commentary-u-dot-s-dot-airlines-make-sure-your-partners-are-safe

"World Air Cargo Forecasts, 2014-2015." The Boeing Company. Retrieved July 29, 2015 from http://www.boeing.com/resources/boeingdotcom/commercial/about-our-market/cargo-market-detail-wacf/download-report/assets/pdfs/wacf.pdf

Zhang, Q. December 1, 2010. "Comprehensive Review of Airport Business Models." Airports Council International. http://aci-asiapac.aero/ (accessed July 27, 2015).

Zeithaml, V.A., L.L. Berry, and A. Parasuraman. 1988. "Communications and Controls Processes in the Delivery of Service Quality." *Journal of Marketing* 52, no. 2, p. 36.

Index

OTHER TITLES IN OUR INDUSTRY PROFILES COLLECTION

Donald Stengel, California State University, Fresno, Editor

- *A Profile of the Hospitality Industry* by Betsy Bender Stringam and Charles Partlow
- *A Profile of the Farm Machinery Industry: Helping Farmers Feed the World* by Dawn M. Drake
- *A Profile of the Automobile and Motor Vehicle Industry: Innovation, Transformation, Globalization* by James M. Rubenstein
- *A Profile of the Software Industry: Emergence, Ascendance, Risks, and Rewards* by Sandra A. Slaughter
- *A Profile of the Performing Arts Industry: Culture and Commerce* by David H. Gaylin

Business Expert Press has over 30 collection in business subjects such as finance, marketing strategy, sustainability, public relations, economics, accounting, corporate communications, and many others. For more information about all our collections, please visit www.businessexpertpress.com/collections.

Business Expert Press is actively seeking collection editors as well as authors. For more information about becoming an BEP author or collection editor, please visit http://www.businessexpertpress.com/author

Announcing the Business Expert Press Digital Library

Concise e-books business students need for classroom and research

This book can also be purchased in an e-book collection by your library as

- a one-time purchase,
- that is owned forever,
- allows for simultaneous readers,
- has no restrictions on printing, and
- can be downloaded as PDFs from within the library community.

Our digital library collections are a great solution to beat the rising cost of textbooks. E-books can be loaded into their course management systems or onto students' e-book readers.
The **Business Expert Press** digital libraries are very affordable, with no obligation to buy in future years. For more information, please visit **www.businessexpertpress.com/librarians**. To set up a trial in the United States, please email **sales@businessexpertpress.com**.

Printed in the USA
CPSIA information can be obtained
at www.ICGtesting.com
JSHW010335190924
69888JS00009B/162

9 781606 495544